The
Sunshine Laws

Board of Directors

President .... Albert W. Hawk, *Livingston-Steuben-Wyoming BOCES*
Vice President .... Pamela Betheil, *Longwood*
Vice President .... Gordon S. Purrington, *Guilderland*
Treasurer .... Earl Lumley, *St. Lawrence-Lewis BOCES*
Immediate Past President .... Judith H. Katz, *Erie 1 BOCES*
Area 1 .... Alison Hyde, *Hopevale*
Area 2 .... Caroline "Tarry" Shipley, *Canandaigua*
Area 3 .... Delores Ackerman, *WellsvilleCattaraugus-Allegany-Erie-Wyoming BOCES*
Area 4 .... Daniel F. Schultz, *Skaneateles*
Area 5 .... Kenneth J. Kazanjian, *New Hartford*
Area 6 .... Earl Lumley, *St. Lawrence-Lewis BOCES*
Area 7 .... Gordon S. Purrington, *Guilderland*
Area 8 .... Josephine Watts, *Hamilton-Fulton-Montgomery BOCES*
Area 9 .... James Loveday, *Arlington*
Area 10 .... Georgine J. Hyde, *East Ramapo*
Area 11 .... Iris Wolfson, *Nassau BOCES*
Area 12 .... Pamela Betheil, *Longwood*
City of New York .... *Vacant*
Large City School Boards .... L. Kathleen LaMorte, *Yonkers*
National School Boards Association .... Arlene R. Penfield
NSBA President
Clinton-Essex-Warren-Washington BOCES (Non-voting)

Staff

Executive Director .... Louis Grumet
Deputy Executive Director .... James V. Vetro
Director, Policy, Risk Management
  and Employee Relations Services .... Robert J. Rader, Esq.
Employee Relations Consultant .... Edward R. Tetreault, Esq.
Policy Resources Assistant .... Karen A. Prescott
Policy Consultant .... Michael Bieber, Esq.
General Counsel .... Jay Worona, Esq.
Director of Publications .... William J. Pape
Editor .... Elizabeth Coccio
Graphic Artist .... Terri Lawlor

The Sunshine Laws

A Handbook for
School Board Members

New York State
School Boards Association

Contents

Part Two. The Freedom of Information Law

Part Three. The Family Educational Rights and Privacy Act

Foreword

The public's right to know about the business of government in New York State has long been one of the fundamental doctrines supporting our concept of democracy. Shedding light on the Open Meetings Law, the Freedom of Information Law, and the Family Educational Rights and Privacy Act, *The Sunshine Laws* will help bring the school districts of the people closer to the people. This handbook demystifies the workings of school districts and brings increased credibility and accountability to local school district governance.

As Secretary of State, I was a member of the Committee on Public Access to Records, now known as the Committee on Open Government. My experience on that committee, as well as my other experiences in public service, have reinforced my belief in the need for increased access to government processes.

For school board members and members of the public, this handbook provides an invaluable guide to better understanding of these laws and processes.

Mario M. Cuomo
Governor
New York State

Preface

Believing, as did U. S. Supreme Court justice Louis Brandeis, that "sunlight is the best disinfectant," New York State and the federal government enacted several laws in the 1970s aimed at opening further the processes of local government to public scrutiny. The Open Meetings Law, the Freedom of Information Law and the Family Educational Rights and Privacy Act, which we have termed the sunshine laws, are now part of the accepted practice of how boards of education conduct business.

Rather than view the sunshine laws as restrictions on school boards, we believe these statutes help define the relationship of boards to the public who elected them and to whom boards are ultimately accountable. Seen from this point of view, the sunshine laws are central to ensuring that an important tenet of local government be advanced: The people have the right to know what their governments are doing and how they are doing it.

New York State's Open Meetings Law prescribes the procedures under which meetings of public bodies, such as school boards, are held. The Freedom of Information Law defines which records must be made available and under what conditions they are to be made so. Both laws were enacted on the premise that proceedings of school boards and the records maintained by districts should be open to public view, with certain specified limitations.

The Family Educational Rights and Privacy Act is discussed in this handbook, although, to some extent, it is designed to prohibit the disclosure of certain educational records. We have included it because at least as it pertains to parents, students and others, it encourages disclosure.

The Sunshine Laws is designed to provide practical advice to board members, administrators and others who must carry out their responsibilities within the framework of these laws. We hope this unique publication may answer many of your questions about the public's right to know.

Louis Grumet
Executive Director
New York State School Boards Association

PART 1

The Open Meetings Law

1. Introduction

New York State's Open Meetings Law gives the public the right to attend meetings of public bodies, such as school boards, listen to the debates and observe the decision-making process in action. The law, which went into effect in 1977,[1] also requires public bodies to conduct any public business "in the sunshine," so that decisions and debates are open to public view and scrutiny.

The Open Meetings Law is to be given a broad and liberal interpretation to achieve the purposes for which it was enacted, as stated in the statute's legislative declaration: "It is essential to the maintenance of a democratic society that the public business be performed in an open and public manner and that the citizens of this state be fully aware of and able to observe the performance of public officials and attend and listen to the deliberations and decisions that go into the making of public policy."[2] It is clear that the Legislature, by enacting the Open Meetings Law, intended to affect the entire decision-making process, not merely formal vote taking, because it is the "deliberative process which is at the core of the Open Meetings Law."[3]

However, as with most laws, the statutory language of the Open Meetings Law does not address every aspect of every possible situation, and the law is therefore subject to judicial interpretation. Even such judicial interpretation has struggled with assessing the advantages and disadvantages of the law. In a landmark decision in 1978 concerning the Open Meetings Law, New York State's highest court, the New York State Court of Appeals, noted, "The fact of the matter is that neither public nor private meetings of governmental bodies are inherently desirable or undesirable. Whichever kind of meeting is permitted or required, there are . . . offsetting losses and gains. The evaluation and balancing of the factors are ultimately, within the framework of the present statute and the issues as presented, for the State Legislature and not the courts."[4]

The Committee on Open Government

The Committee on Open Government is an advisory body established in 1974, pursuant to the enactment of New York State's Freedom of Information Law.[5] The committee is composed of 11 members, five from state government and six from the general public. The committee's five members from state government include the lieutenant governor, the secretary of state, the commissioner of general services, the director of the budget, and one elected local government official appointed by the gover-

The authors wish to acknowledge the support and assistance of Robert J. Freeman, Executive Director of the Committee on Open Government, in preparing this handbook.

nor. At least two of the six public members must be or have been representatives of the news media.

The committee's main function is to provide written or oral advice interpreting the Open Meetings Law, as well as the Freedom of Information Law and the Personal Privacy Protection Law.[6] The committee prepares written advisory opinions at the request of any government agency, the news media or member of the general public.

The Committee on Open Government has no power to enforce the laws it regulates; instead, the Legislature has delegated this responsibility to the courts. Although the committee's advice is often given considerable deference by the courts, it clearly is not binding on them.[7] The New York State Court of Appeals has held that although a citizen may at any time resort to the Committee on Open Government for an advisory opinion, the weight of such opinion obtains from the strength of the opinion's reasoning and analysis, rather from the fact that it was rendered by the committee.[8] Nevertheless, the committee's opinions can be influential in swaying public opinion on any sunshine law issue, and they have been cited in numerous court decisions.

Access to Meetings

The Open Meetings Law stipulates "every meeting of a public body shall be open to the general public, except that an executive session of such body may be called and business transacted thereat in accordance with section [105] of this article." This requirement applies to all types of such meetings, including regular, annual, special and reorganizational meetings.[9]

The requirement also calls for meetings to be accessible to the public. Although the Open Meetings Law does not require that meetings be held within district boundaries, a court may look unfavorably upon meetings held in remote locations when deliberating whether such a meeting was held in order to avoid the public and the media.

In addition, the Open Meetings Law requires public bodies to make "all reasonable efforts to ensure that meetings are held in facilities that permit barrier-free physical access" to disabled persons.[10] State and federal laws require school districts and other owners of public facilities to conform to building construction standards designed to ensure barrier-free access to the disabled.[11] The provisions of the Public Buildings Law are enforced against school districts by the State Education Department.[12] They apply to new construction as well as to existing buildings undergoing renovations.[13]

State law also makes it the duty of each public officer responsible for the scheduling of any public hearing "to make reasonable efforts to ensure that such hearings are held in facilities that permit barrier-free access to the physically-handicapped." These laws do not impose an inflexible requirement of barrier-free access; they only require public bodies to make "reasonable efforts" toward that end.[14]

Definitions

The Open Meetings Law defines the terms meeting, public body and executive session.

Meeting

" 'Meeting' means the official convening of a public body for the purpose of conducting public business."[15]

Under the original law, *meeting* meant the formal convening of a public body for the purpose of officially transacting public business. However, in a decision rendered in 1978, the Appellate Division, a middle-level state court, held that any convening of a quorum of a public body for the purpose of discussing public business is a "meeting" subject to the Open Meetings Law, whether or not there is an intent to take action and regardless of the manner in which a meeting may be characterized.[16]

An amendment made to the Open Meetings Law in 1979 revised the definition of *meeting* in accordance with the decision, redefining the term as the "official convening of a public body for the purpose of conducting public business." Note that the memorandum in support of the legislation indicates the insertion of the word "official" was intended "to avoid inadvertently including chance meetings and social gatherings" within the scope of the law. For a further discussion of meetings covered or exempt under the Open Meetings Law, see chapter 3.[17]

Public Body

" 'Public body' means any entity, for which a quorum is required in order to transact public business and which consists of two or more members, performing a governmental function for the state or for an agency or department thereof, or for a public corporation as defined in section sixty-six of the general construction law, or committee or subcommittee or similar body of such public body."[18]

Because school districts are defined as "public corporations" under state law, boards of education and their committees and subcommittees are clearly subject to the provisions of the Open Meetings Law. A board of cooperative educational services (BOCES) also would fall within the definition of a "public body" subject to this law.[19]

Executive Session

" 'Executive session' means that portion of a meeting not open to the general public."[20]

It is important to note that an executive session is defined as a *portion* of an open meeting during which the public may be excluded. However, an executive session does not constitute, and may not be regarded as, a *separate* meeting. Requirements of the Open Meetings Law pertaining to executive sessions are addressed in chapter 6.

2. Covered Bodies

The Open Meetings Law applies to all public bodies. School districts, as "municipal corporations," are defined as public bodies under state law.[1] In addition, committees and subcommittees are specifically included under the definition of "public body."[2] Hence, school boards as well as their committees and subcommittees, all fall within the framework of this law.

Boards of Education

School boards are considered public bodies within the meaning and subject to the provisions of the Open Meetings Law.[3] All school board meetings convened to transact public business must be open and accessible to the public, except those "executive sessions" properly convened pursuant to section 105 of the law.[4] This requirement has been extended to include committees and subcommittees of such public bodies. While it is clear that not every assemblage of the members of a public body was intended to fall within the scope of the Open Meetings Law, it is settled that informal conferences, agenda sessions and work sessions do invoke the provisions of the statute when a quorum is present and when the topics for discussion and decision are such that would otherwise arise at a regular meeting.[5] Such meetings are covered more fully in chapter 3.

Standing Committees

When the Open Meetings Law was originally enacted, school board standing committees were excluded from its provisions because such committees did not fall within the definition of the term *public body* and were not empowered to "transact" any public business.[6] However, in 1979, the law was amended to specifically include committees and subcommittees within the definition of *public body*. Thus, it is clear that any school board standing committee that arranges to meet with a quorum of its members present for the purpose of transacting public business is subject to the provisions of the Open Meetings Law.

Advisory Committees

Early court decisions held that it was not necessary for an entity to have binding authority for it to be considered a public body, because it was covered by the Open Meetings Law "if its determinations affect the public and eventually obtain substance in official form."[7] However, recently courts have held that the essential factor in determining the applicability of the Open Meetings Law is whether or not the entity is *performing a governmental function*, not simply *conducting public business*.

A number of Appellate Division cases suggest that because the mere giving of advice is not the performance of a governmental function, such committees do not "transact any public business" and, therefore, do not perform a "governmental function" analogous to a "public body" under the law.[8]

It is also relevant to consider whether or not the entity in question specifically requires a "quorum" in order to conduct its business, because it has been held that entities given no real power or authority (such as "advisory committees") are not subject to the statutory quorum required of entities that perform a public duty.[9] Such a determination is important because the requirement of a quorum is one of the statutory characteristics of a "public body" under the Open Meetings Law.[10] These cases suggest that because such committees and subcommittees lack the right to exercise some part of the power of the sovereign, the individual members of such entities, while functioning in that capacity, are not public officers and are not members of a "public body" subject to the provisions of the law. On the other hand, this apparent trend should not be interpreted as a rule. The state's highest court has yet to rule specifically on this issue.

The Committee on Open Government has issued numerous advisory opinions holding that committees and subcommittees consisting *solely* of members of a governing body, such as a board of education, perform a governmental function and are thus subject to the Open Meetings Law. The committee has also stated that advisory bodies that *do not* consist of members of a governing body, such as citizens' advisory bodies, are not subject to the law.[11] The committee has gone so far as to suggest to the Legislature that the definition of *public bodies* be amended to clarify the legislative intent as to whether or not advisory bodies are to be included within that definition. The Legislature has not acted on this suggestion.

None of the decisions cited above deal specifically with entities that have the authority to recommend but which include members of a governing body such as a board of education. At this juncture, based on recent court decisions, such committees do not appear to be governed by the Open Meetings Law; however, based upon the noted trend toward opening meetings to greater public scrutiny, we believe it is advisable for school boards to adopt a policy permitting public access to such meetings.

3. Covered Meetings

In general, any time a quorum of a public body gathers for the purpose of discussing public business, the meeting must be open to the public, whether or not there is an intent to take action and regardless of the manner in which the gathering may be characterized.

Public bodies may not escape public view by claiming they did not formally convene when, in fact, a meeting had taken place during which business of public interest was discussed.[1] The courts have recognized that the Legislature, by enacting the Open Meetings Law, intended to affect the entire decision-making process and not merely formal vote taking, as it is the "deliberative process that is at the core of the Open Meetings Law."[2]

However, not every assemblage of members of a public body is a meeting under the Open Meetings Law.[3] The law applies to "official" convenings, so chance meetings, social gatherings and other casual encounters by members do not fall within its purview (see "Retreats," p. 11). On the other hand, informal conferences, agenda sessions, work sessions and other private meetings *do* invoke the provisions of the statute "when a quorum is present and when the topics for discussion and decision are such as would otherwise arise at a regular meeting."[4] "Joint" or "infrequent" meetings are not excepted from these requirements.[5]

In one noteworthy case, the Appellate Division reasoned, "If the legislative intent was to permit public bodies to convene at gatherings that they themselves interpreted to be informal, during which they could discuss the business of the public body, then the New York State Legislature would not have provided for executive sessions. The very mechanism for an executive session, in and of itself, suggests that the Legislature wanted to provide for the possibility of a private working session in the absence of the public eye, but only under the express conditions and enumerated purposes contained therein."[6]

Thus, it is clear that although the presence of a quorum of board members at a meeting may prove to be a determining factor in deciding whether a violation of the Open Meetings Law occurred, it is of no significance that formal action was not taken at such a meeting.[7] If a quorum is lacking, there is no violation.[8] However, once the presence of a quorum is planned or actually obtained, the session or meeting is automatically covered under the Open Meetings Law.[9]

If a quorum of a public body should meet to conduct public business, this would constitute a meeting under the terms of the Open Meetings Law; therefore, based on the direction given by the courts, meetings of board members classified as "informal conferences," "agenda sessions," "work sessions" and other private meetings do invoke the provisions of the Open Meetings Law *when a quorum is present* and *when the topics for discussion are such as would otherwise arise at a regular meeting.*[10]

Work Sessions

Work sessions, also referred to as *study sessions or planning sessions*, generally refer to informal board meetings held so board members can discuss various topics of interest, gather information and weigh alternatives in preparation for an actual board meeting.

In a landmark case in 1978 dealing directly with the issue of work sessions and similar gatherings, the New York State Court of Appeals, the state's highest court, unanimously held that such sessions are "meetings" subject to the requirements of the Open Meetings Law. Before this ruling, public bodies contended that such informal gatherings held only for the purpose of discussion and not with the intent to take action, fell outside the scope and objectives of the Open Meetings Law. The court stated that any gathering of a quorum of a public body for the purpose of conducting public business constitutes a "meeting" subject to the Open Meetings Law, *whether or not there is an intent to take action* and *regardless of the manner in which the gathering might be characterized.*[11]

Such judicial interpretation makes it evident that public bodies intending to hold such "work sessions" must do so in accordance with the provisions of the Open Meetings Law.

Agenda Sessions

An *agenda session* is sometimes used by boards as a premeeting device to consider and shape the agenda's eventual form so that the board can function more efficiently during the actual meeting.

As with work sessions and other informal conferences, the courts have held that meetings denoted as agenda sessions, at which a quorum of a public body is present for the purpose of transacting public business, fall within the purview of the Open Meetings Law. The Court of Appeals has reasoned that this is because such sessions permit "the crystallization of secret decisions to a point just short of ceremonial acceptance."[12]

Briefing Sessions

Similarly, there is no legislative exception to the Open Meetings Law for *briefing sessions* or *premeeting gatherings*. In addition, a school board's weekly planning sessions have been held to be meetings under the Open Meetings Law.[13]

The Committee on Open Government advises that a debriefing session conducted following a school board meeting in order to allow board members to critique one another's performance, discuss what went well or not well at the meeting and analyze how board behavior could be improved is a meeting covered by the Open Meetings Law. The committee reasons that any convening of a public body, such as a school board, held for the purpose of discussing or conducting public business constitutes a meeting subject to the Open Meetings Law in all respects, whether or not there is an intent to take action and regardless of the manner in which a gathering may be characterized. Thus, if a quorum of the board meets, such a gathering would clearly fall within the definition of meeting that appears in the Open Meetings Law.

Retreats

School boards sometimes hold closed-session programs, referred to as *retreats*, for the purpose of building teamwork and improving board effectiveness. Typically, such retreats are not designed to encourage school board members to "act upon" or even discuss topics that "would otherwise arise at a regular meeting."[14]

Such retreats are generally designed to enable school board members to consider their overall effectiveness, determine their strengths and weaknesses and identify potential areas for improvement. The program is held in a retreat setting to allow participating school board members to express their opinions candidly. Essentially, if the program is successful, participants will feel encouraged to return to their meeting tables *in public* and perform their roles more effectively.

Although the specific issue of school board members attending such retreats has not yet been addressed by New York State's courts, such attendance, for the limited purposes stated above, would not appear to violate the Open Meetings Law. On the other hand, if school board members discuss matters of public concern at such retreats (for example, particular policies and/or particular subjects in which the community has an interest), such a meeting would have to be open to the public pursuant to the provisions of the law. Accordingly, although the Open Meetings Law does not specify where meetings may be held, if board members intend to discuss matters of public concern at such retreats, courts may require these meetings to be held at a location reasonably accessible to members of the public.

Exempt Meetings

Not every assembly of members of a public body was intended to fall within the scope of the Open Meetings Law. Section 108 of the law exempts certain matters. Because the law does not *require* these matters to be discussed in executive session, they may, at the discretion of the public body, be discussed in open session–although this is not recommended. If such matters are discussed in executive session, they need not be included in the minutes.

Judicial and quasi-judicial proceedings, together with deliberations of political committees and caucuses, are specifically exempted from the requirements of the statute.[15] A board of education acts in a quasi-judicial capacity when it hears testimony, weighs evidence and makes a determination affecting the rights of individuals that would be analogous to one made by a court. A school board may act in such capacity when involved in hearing a case of a student's suspension or an employee grievance; in such instances, the meeting need not be open. The commissioner of education has held that a board of education is required only to affirm or modify a superintendent's decision concerning a student suspension in open session.[16]

Matters made confidential by federal or state law are also exempt from the Open Meetings Law.[17] For example, because a school's attorney enjoys an attorney-client relationship with the board, if the board seeks his or her advice, regarding, for example, the discussion of legal action against a board member, such communication would be privileged under New York's Civil Practice Law and Rules (CPLR). This would be a matter made confidential by state law and would fall within the enumerated exemptions contained in the Open Meetings Law.[18]

The federal Family Educational Rights and Privacy Act (FERPA), commonly known as the Buckley Amendment, protects the privacy of student records and allows disclosure only under limited circumstances.[19] The act prohibits school districts that accept federal funds from disclosing personally identifiable information about a student to any person, organization or agency, other than designated school staff, without the prior written consent of his or her parents, describing the specific information to be released.[20] As such, a school board's discussion of a particular student's records would be a matter involving personal privacy made confidential by federal law and would fall within the exemptions contained in the Open Meetings Law.[21]

Another example would involve the disclosure of information pertaining to children with handicapping conditions. The evaluation and placement of all children with handicapping conditions are made confidential pursuant to the Commissioner's Regulation and FERPA.[22] This applies to all Committee on Special Education meetings, hearings conducted pursuant to Article 89 of the Education Law and to any portion of a meeting during which the evaluation of a child with a handicapping condition is to be discussed. The minutes of any session discussing the placement of any child with a handicapping condition should reflect only the vote taken; neither the handicapped student's name nor any other personally identifiable information should be disclosed. School boards may find it helpful to use case numbers that correlate the action taken at the meeting to the student's school record file. As such, this would be a matter made confidential by both state and federal law and therefore exempted from discussion in an open meeting.

Such matters, except for the voting of charges against a tenured teacher under section 3020-a and matters pertaining to the placement of children with handicapping conditions, need not be included in the minutes and may be discussed in closed session.[23]

Casual encounters and social gatherings by board members clearly do not fall within the Open Meetings Law's consideration.[24] These may include retreats, meals and chance meetings. Again, it is important to remember that if the topic of discussion during one of these meetings becomes one that would otherwise arise at a regular meeting, such a meeting would have to open with proper notice given to the public. In one case, the court held that a "dinner gathering" held between two open meetings, during which discussion of the budget was incidental to general social intercourse, did not violate the Open Meetings Law. However, the same court found a technical violation of the law occurred when, at a "luncheon gathering," staff reported to the board on cutting expenses and increasing anticipated income.[25]

Such judicial interpretations clearly illustrate it is not the name given to the meeting, but the topics discussed or decided, together with whether a quorum of members is present, that determine whether a board must comply with the Open Meetings Law. The courts have noted that to ensure the realization of the purpose of the Open Meetings Law, the statutory exemptions discussed above are usually narrowly, not expansively, construed.[26]

4. Notice of Meetings

The Open Meetings Law requires notice of the time and place of all meetings to be given to the public and news media before every meeting.[1] In addition, the Education Law requires that proper notice be given to school board members and sets forth the requirements governing the frequency of meetings.[2]

Public Notice

The Open Meetings Law requires that if a meeting is scheduled at least a week in advance, notice of its time and place must be given to the public and the news media not less than 72 hours before the meeting. Such notice must be conspicuously posted in one or more designated public locations.[3]

If a meeting is scheduled less than a week in advance, notice of the time and place of the meeting must be given to the public and the news media "to the extent practicable" at a reasonable time before the meeting. Once again, such a notice must be conspicuously posted.[4] However, it does not have to include information on the business to be transacted.

Compliance with the Open Meetings Law's notice requirements is important because courts have the discretion to invalidate any and all action taken at a meeting where it is proven that such notice requirements had been violated. In one case, a lower court held that a school board's posting of one typewritten notice on the central office's bulletin board announcing a specially called board meeting violated the notice requirements of the Open Meetings Law because the notice was not given "to the extent practicable" to the news media and was not conspicuously posted in one or more designated public locations before the meeting. The Appellate Division affirmed the lower court's invalidation of all of the action taken at the meeting by finding the board's violation was intentional in the absence of an adequate explanation for the last-minute, improperly publicized meeting.[5]

On the other hand, courts have sometimes refused to invalidate action taken at a meeting where the defective notice was merely "technically inadequate" or otherwise "unintentional."[6] In another case, the Appellate Division ruled on a situation where notice of three special meetings–all of which were scheduled less than one week in advance–was given to the local newspaper *and* posted in the town clerk's office in the same place where notice of the regular board meetings was posted and on the same days as each of the three special meetings was scheduled. It held the notice was provided "within a reasonable time" prior to the meetings and did not justify invalidation of the action taken at the meeting. The court reasoned, "Assuming . . . that this does not constitute full compliance with the Open Meetings Law, we conclude in the exercise of our discretion that under all of the circumstances . . . invalidation . . . is not appropriate."[7]

What is reasonable will, of course, depend upon the circumstances, but notice of an impending meeting certainly should be given as promptly as possible after the decision to hold it has been made. Whether the notice is given to the news media in writing or orally (by telephone or otherwise), the person giving the notice should make a written record of the fact promptly and file it with the records of the public body. Proof that notice of a meeting was given will be important if the action taken by the board during that meeting should be challenged on the grounds that the notice had been inadequate.

Board Members

Section 1606(1) of the Education Law states, "The board must meet for the transaction of business in accordance with notice of time and place." Section 1606(3) further requires that a board member calling a special or emergency meeting of the board notify all of the other members at least 24 hours in advance of the meeting.

Written notice to board members is not required. Serving notice by mail will be sufficient if the notice is sent to provide the required 24-hour notice by ordinary mail. Although the notice to the board members generally includes a statement of the specific business to be transacted at the special meeting, this is not required by law.

In an emergency, the 24-hour notice may be waived by unanimous consent of all board members. If such a situation should arise, it would be advisable for each member who attends the meeting to sign a waiver-of-notice form and to have a record of such waiver entered in the minutes of the meeting.

The commissioner of education has held that a majority of a board of education may not dispense with notice of a board meeting to other board members. All members of a board may reasonably expect to be given notice of meetings and an opportunity to participate in the decisions of the board.[8] However, if reasonable efforts are made to notify the board members of a special meeting, the meeting should not be set aside on the grounds that proper notice was not given.[9] Of course, what is "reasonable" is a question of fact to be determined by consideration of the particular circumstances of each case.

Frequency of Meetings

New York State Education Law prescribes the minimum number of regular meetings a board of education must hold. Regular meetings must be held at a time, date and place established by the board at its annual reorganizational meeting. Any deviation from the established schedule may be made at subsequent meetings, so long as the statutory notice requirements are satisfied.

The boards of education of common, union free and central school districts must hold regular meetings at least once in each quarter of the year.[10] Most boards meet at least once each month.

In city school districts, regular board meetings must be held at least once each month.[11]

Special Meetings

A *special meeting* is a board meeting usually called for emergency or urgent purposes, or as agreed upon at previous regular or special meetings of the board. Although ordinarily a special meeting is held to consider a single item of business, the law does not prohibit action on other matters during its course.

The Education Law provides that a special meeting may be called by any board member by giving not less than 24 hours' notice to all board members of the time and place of the meeting.[12] However, such a requirement may be waived by unanimous consent of the board's members (see "Board Members," p. 16). Boards of city school districts are required by law to prescribe a method for calling special meetings.[13]

If a special meeting is scheduled at least one week in advance, the Open Meetings Law requires that notice of the time and place of the meeting be given to the public and the news media not less than 72 hours before the meeting. When a meeting is scheduled less than one week in advance, notice must be given to the public and the news media "to the extent practicable" at a reasonable time before the meeting. In both instances, the law requires that notice be conspicuously posted in one or more designated public locations. The notice to the public does not have to include notice of the business that will be transacted.[14]

5. Procedures at Meetings

Rules of Order

Rules of order are written rules of parliamentary procedure formally adopted by a board to govern the conduct of board meetings. They generally relate to the orderly transaction of business in meetings and to the duties of officers. Their purpose is to expedite the smooth functioning of board meetings by providing a framework for resolving questions of procedure that occasionally arise. Formally adopted rules of procedure are helpful in clarifying disagreement or misunderstanding on points of order that can affect the outcome of substantive issues.

Although not required by law or regulation, boards generally adopt either a standard reference or a specific set of rules to facilitate the conduct of their meetings. The most common method by which a board adopts a suitable set of rules is to include in its policies a provision designating the current edition of a standard manual of parliamentary procedure as its chosen authority. The best known and most commonly used reference is *Robert's Rules of Order, Newly Revised;*[1] however, there are other references that may be adopted by a board (for example, *Parliamentary Procedure at a Glance*, by O. Garfield Jones).

In addition, a board may adopt special rules of order to supplement or modify the rules contained in its specified reference. The rules of order a board adopts are binding on it, except where they conflict with a policy or other special rule or any applicable law or regulation. For example, although *Robert's Rules of Order* generally provides for the suspension of rules by a two-thirds vote, the commissioner of education has ruled a board of education has no authority to require a vote in excess of a simple majority to take such action; a simple majority vote is sufficient. Thus, the adoption of a rule requiring more than a simple majority would be invalidated by the applicable law.[2]

Whenever a board wishes to act contrary to one or more of its adopted rules of order, it may, by majority vote, adopt a motion for amendment, alteration, correction or repeal of the rules, or suspension of their operation for the meeting. The power to suspend the rules does not apply to any procedures required by law governing the conduct of board meetings.

Rules of order are an invaluable tool for the conduct of a board meeting. Whether a board chooses to adopt a standard reference or rules of its own, the procedures established should be flexible enough to allow the president to direct the meeting in an orderly and efficient manner.

Agendas

The Open Meetings Law does not require an agenda to be prepared or disseminated to board members or the public before a regular or special meeting. On the other hand, good business practice would indicate the use of an agenda at regular board meetings.[3] A good agenda is often the framework on which a board meeting is constructed. It should serve as a useful tool to prepare participants for the business to be addressed and helps guide them through it during the meeting. Such a tool is extremely important to most boards, which must balance efforts to hold productive, efficient meetings against attempts to remain receptive to the concerns of their constituents, all in a considerably limited amount of available meeting time.

A board may prescribe procedures for the preparation and dissemination of the agenda of regular meetings to board members and the public. Preparing and disseminating an agenda in advance of a board meeting allows board members to become familiar with the particular subjects to be discussed and helps to ensure an efficiently conducted meeting. One efficient method of preparing an agenda is to designate one person to be responsible for it. For example, a school board may decide that the superintendent, board president or clerk will prepare the agenda. As an alternative, the board may establish a separate agenda committee or involve a combination of individuals in preparing it.

Whatever method is chosen, provision should be made for the agenda to be disseminated to the superintendent, the president and members of the board at a specified time before each meeting (for example, not less than 24 hours before the meeting). A list of proposed resolutions, motions and statements of policy may be prepared to expedite the meeting. Where possible, backup material should be sent to board members with the agenda. Most school districts provide individual board members with copies of these materials.

Boards may want to make copies of the agenda available to the public at a designated place before the meeting. The agenda may allow for recognition and comments by individuals; however, such comments may be limited to matters presented on the agenda should the board deem it necessary. If a board determines that public participation is compromising the productivity of meetings, one way to resolve the issue may be to have members, school district employees and citizens propose items for discussion to whomever sets the proposed agenda (this is usually the superintendent), who may, in turn, discuss them with the president. The president may include the items on the agenda if they are appropriate. The board also may require individuals who wish to propose such items to submit them in writing to the superintendent a designated period of time before the applicable board meeting.

A board may prescribe a format for its agendas for regular and special meetings. A standard format is often helpful in maintaining efficiency and order during board meetings. The person designated to prepare an agenda should also be responsible for arranging the order of its items in accordance with the established format. The board may choose to arrange the standard format for the agenda of regular meetings in any one of a number of appropriate ways. However, the standard format of a special meeting generally will be limited to the call to order, determination of quorum and discussion of the specific item or items of business at hand.

The board also may resolve that matters not included in the original agenda may be added before or during the meeting at the request of any member or upon a majority vote of the board. Omission of appropriate board business from the agenda need not preclude any action on it. Alternatively, the board may resolve that official action not occur unless such action has been properly scheduled for discussion. It probably is not in a board's interest to limit its right to act on any and all matters that have not been placed on the agenda before the meeting; however, there are some matters that, as a general rule, should be voted upon only after sufficient notice has been given to all members of the board so that they can acquaint themselves with the subject. Matters of policy often require this consideration, as does adoption of a budget. In some cases the board may wish to prescribe more than one regular meeting at which an item is scheduled before a formal vote may be taken. This is a common requirement for the adoption, amendment or appeal of a board's policy.

School boards, by establishing appropriate requirements for the preparation and dissemination of agendas, have the inherent ability to manage their business meetings in an efficient, orderly and democratic manner. To accomplish this, boards should establish requirements to enable them to retain both procedural and substantive control over their meetings while they provide the public with a reasonable opportunity to participate.

Public Participation

The Open Meetings Law gives the public the right to attend meetings of public bodies, listen to the deliberations and decisions that go into the making of public policy and watch the decision-making process in action.[4] However, the law is silent with respect to public participation, so it is clear that although a public body may *permit* an individual to speak at its open meetings, it is *not required* to do so. On the other hand, the commissioner of education has recognized the responsibility of boards of education "to keep the residents informed and to provide channels of communication through which residents are encouraged to express their opinions on school matters."[5]

As specified earlier, a board may invite public discussion and comment by implementing an agenda format that provides an opportunity for its constituents to express their concerns for the district. However, some boards find that the absence of an established time limit for public participation often leads to lack of order and control over their meetings. School board members should realize that although its board meetings are held in public, they are not public meetings in the same sense as a traditional town board meeting, where each resident has the right to speak.

One method of recognizing public participation is to set aside a portion of regular board meetings for persons who wish to address the board about specific items on the agenda. As an alternative, a board may choose to limit public participation to a specific number of meetings per year. A board may establish an overall time limit on the length of such public participation periods. The board may require written notice by a specified time before the meeting from individuals who wish to address items on the agenda. Another common restriction is not to allow substitution of speakers.

Boards may impose reasonable limits on the time, manner and content of such participation. Such limits are beneficial in maintaining a board's efficiency, productivity and control.

Although the protection of freedom of speech guaranteed by the First Amendment would dictate that the board not discriminate against speakers based on the content of their speech, the meeting need not become an open forum where every person expresses an opinion on every matter. Verbal attacks on individual board or staff members should not be tolerated at board meetings. As part of board policy, rules may be established forbidding interruption, slanderous remarks or name-calling. Items of business introduced from the floor, including but not limited to intraschool and personnel issues, should be ruled out of order and not acted upon at the meeting.

A member of the public who wishes to speak at a board meeting should be recognized by the president first, identify himself or herself, any organization he or she may be representing at the meeting and the agenda topic he or she wishes to discuss. Comments should be as brief as possible and related to matters on the agenda. The board need not establish a required procedure for response to public comments. Where individual items are concerned, the president may answer questions, refer questions to the board or staff members for reply, or reserve consideration for later response.

The public should realize that speaking about items on the agenda and making public comments at board meetings is a *privilege*, not a right. By prescribing reasonable controls on public participation, boards can effectively reduce or eliminate non-productive meeting time and conduct business in a more orderly and efficient manner.

Tape Recorders and Cameras

The Open Meetings Law is silent with respect to the use of tape recorders and other broadcasting or televising devices at public meetings, but rules restricting the use of tape recorders have been the subject of various court actions. The leading case involved a school board that adopted a resolution prohibiting the use of all tape recorders at its public meetings.[6] The Appellate Division, the highest-level New York State court that ruled on the issue, held there was no justifiable basis for prohibiting the use of unobtrusive, hand-held tape-recording devices at public meetings of a board of education, "particularly when viewed in light of the legislative scheme embodied in the Open Meetings Law[,] which was enacted and designed to enable members of the public to 'listen to the deliberations and decisions that go into the making of public policy.'"[7] The court reasoned that "those who attend such meetings, and who decide to freely speak out and voice their opinions, fully realize that their comments and remarks are being made in a public forum. The argument that members of the public should be protected from the use of their words, and that they have some sort of privacy interest in their own comments, is therefore wholly specious. . . . While Education Law §1709 (1) authorizes a board of education to adopt bylaws and rules for its government and operations, this authority is not unbridled. Irrational and unreasonable rules will not be sanctioned."[8] To safeguard against possible abuses, a board may direct that the proceedings be tape-recorded contemporaneously to ensure a reliable, accurate and complete account of what is said at board meetings.

In a similar case, a school board member and a member of the audience were charged with criminal trespass and obstructing governmental administration when they refused to turn off their tape recorders and leave a public meeting of a school board, after being advised that their conduct violated the school board's bylaw against tape-recording such meetings.[9] A lower court judge dismissed the charges on the grounds that the board's bylaw was in violation of the Open Meetings Law, and that the board therefore had no right to ask the individuals to stop recording or to leave the meeting.

These cases overrule earlier authorities that had suggested public bodies could adopt rules generally prohibiting individuals from using tape recorders at an open meeting.[10] It is important to note that many of these earlier opinions predate the enactment of the Open Meetings Law and the availability of unobtrusive, hand-held, cassette-style tape recorders and even cameras.

In a case involving a town board, a newspaper editor was arrested for disorderly conduct for refusing to turn off his tape recorder. After the criminal charge was dismissed, the editor sued the town for false arrest and malicious prosecution. The court stated, "Although [the editor] did apparently have the authority to tape record, in an unobtrusive manner, a public meeting, [he] could not, with intent to cause public inconvenience, annoyance or alarm and without lawful authority, disturb any lawful assembly or meeting of persons."[11]

It is implicit in the courts' opinions that school boards still retain the power to prohibit the use of noisy or otherwise obtrusive tape recorders.

The Committee on Open Government has held this to be the case, as well.[12] Similarly, another opinion of the committee holds that the use of cameras in a manner that detracts from the deliberative process of the meeting may be restricted.[13]

The propriety of policies on other forms of electronic recording such as broadcasting or televising devices has not been addressed by the courts thus far. It is important to remember that courts have repeatedly emphasized the "obtrusiveness" of the tape recorders that were being prohibited. Whether or not this reasoning will apply to other electronic recording methods remains to be seen. Accordingly, in developing a policy regarding the use of cameras and other broadcasting and televising equipment in open meetings, a board should take reasonable steps to ensure that any restrictions or prohibitions on their use have a justifiable basis.

Voting

Although the vote required by any action is prescribed by law, in most instances boards are free to establish their own procedures concerning the method of voting. For example, the board may require that a member requesting to be excused from voting make a brief statement of his or her reason why. The board president may excuse any member who declares a direct personal or pecuniary interest in the matter to be voted upon.

For certain actions, however, the method of voting is also prescribed by law.[14] The Open Meetings Law and Freedom of Information Law require the vote of each member who is present to be recorded in the minutes.[15]

For most items before a board, voting may take place by voice or show of hands without a roll call. The vote need not be taken from board members in alphabetical order. Of course, a roll call could be required by a majority vote of the board, either as standard practice or on any particular item. Many boards provide that a roll call may be taken upon the request of any board member. The board may provide for a written ballot upon request; however, each member's vote must be open and recorded.

A board member may abstain from voting. An abstention indicates neither an affirmative nor a negative vote, but it is sometimes argued that the effect of an abstention is the same as that of a negative vote. This is because the law requires "not less than a majority of the whole number [of a public body] may perform and exercise" the "power, authority or duty" with which they are charged.[16] Therefore, because a majority of the full board must cast an affirmative vote in order to carry a motion, an abstention could have the same *practical effect* as a negative vote. In fact, courts have consistently found that an abstention cannot be counted as an affirmative vote and that action may be taken only by means of an affirmative vote of the majority of the total membership of a public body.[17]

Quorum and Majority

It is relevant to consider whether or not the entity in question specifically requires a *quorum* (a simple majority–more than one-half–of the total number of board members) in order to conduct its business, because a number of recent decisions have held that entities with no real power or authority (for example, advisory committees) are not subject to the statutory quorum required of entities that perform a public duty.[18] In addition, the requirement of a quorum is one of the statutory characteristics of a "public body" under the Open Meetings Law.[19]

The General Construction Law requires the affirmative votes of a majority of the total number of board members to carry any resolution or approve any action, except when the law establishes a higher number or percentage. Therefore, if a meeting is held where only a bare majority of the board is present, final action cannot be taken except by the affirmative vote of all those board members constituting the majority.[20] For example, if a board has a total of nine members, and a majority of five is present at a meeting, legal passage of a resolution would require all five votes. A three-to-two or even a four-to-one vote would not be sufficient.

It is important to note that state law does not authorize a board of education to adopt a policy requiring affirmative votes in excess of those already provided by statute. The commissioner of education has held that one board's policy, which required a simple majority of the board to amend the board's rules or regulations (for example, four votes of a five-member board) was unduly restrictive, outside the statutory authority of the board to adopt and therefore void.[21]

There are instances, however, where the law requires a higher percentage of the total board membership to pass a specific resolution. For example, a person cannot be employed as a teacher if related by blood or marriage to a school board member within the same district unless his or her appointment is approved by a two-thirds majority of the board.[22] Similarly, employment of a board member as school district physician, otherwise prohibited by conflict-of-interest provisions of the law, may be authorized by a two-thirds majority of the board.[23] In addition, the law prohibits the supersession of a textbook by any other textbook within a period of five years from the time of such designation, except upon acceptance by a three-fourths majority of the board.[24]

Telephone Voting

Neither the Open Meetings Law nor any of its numerous judicial interpretations specifically prohibit a board's use of voting by telephone. However, the Committee on Open Government held in one recent advisory opinion that a board's policy authorizing it to conduct regular meetings by means of telephone conferences was *invalid* under the Open Meetings Law. The policy in question specifically provided that "telephone conference board meetings shall constitute a regular meeting for the purpose of dealing with emergencies or when it is not possible to have a quorum of the board assembled in one place."[25]

In so holding, the committee recognized "there is nothing in the Open Meetings Law that would preclude members of a public body from conferring by telephone. However, a series of telephone calls among the members which results in a decision or a meeting held by means of a telephone conference, would in [our] opinion violate the Law." The committee reasoned that the statutory definition of *quorum* suggests that a public body has the capacity to carry out its duties only during "duly convened meetings," and that the term *convening* means "a physical coming together" requiring the assembly of a group in order to constitute a quorum of a public body.[26]

Because it is not yet apparent how the courts will rule on this particular issue, it is advisable for boards to refrain from conducting meetings and/or voting by means of telephonic communications.[27]

Secret Ballots

A school board is clearly prohibited from voting by secret ballot under the Open Meetings Law and the Freedom of Information Law.

In a decision later affirmed by New York State's highest court, the Appellate Division held that voting by secret ballot is improper. The court stated that "when action is taken by a formal vote at open or executive sessions, the Freedom of Information Law and Open Meetings Law both require open voting and a record of the manner in which each member voted."[28]

Minutes

The Open Meetings Law requires minutes of both open meetings and executive sessions to be compiled and made available.

Content

Minutes of an open meeting must consist of "a record or summary all motions, proposals, resolutions and any matter formally voted upon and the vote thereon."[29] Such meetings include informal conferences, work sessions, agenda sessions and other gatherings of a public body for the purpose of transacting public business whenever a quorum is present, whether or not a vote of the members of the public body is taken. If, for example, a quorum of a public body convenes a working session or planning meeting at which it does not intend to take any action but subsequently decides to vote on a motion to enter executive session, minutes indicating such action must be prepared and made available to the public. Although the contents of the minutes may be more expansive than the statutory requirements, a board may properly restrict the contents of minutes of an open meeting to these minimum requirements.

Minutes of an executive session must consist of "a record or summary of the final determination" of any action taken "and the date and vote thereon."[30] If, for example, a public body merely discusses a matter during executive session but takes no action, minutes need not be compiled. However, minutes of any action taken in an executive session by a formal vote must be compiled and made available.

Availability of Records

New York State Education Law provides that the clerk of each school district must maintain a record of the proceedings of all the board's meetings in an official book provided for that purpose.[31]

According to the provisions of the Open Meetings Law and Freedom of Information Law, minutes of meetings of all public bodies must be made available to the public *within two weeks* from the date of the meeting. However, minutes taken at executive sessions must be made available to the public *within one week* from the date of the executive session.[32]

These deadlines apply whether or not the minutes have been formally approved by the board. In most instances, the minutes are approved at the next board meeting. Policy or procedures may be established where minutes are forwarded to board members with the agenda of the next meeting for approval at that meeting. In order to conform to the time frame permitted by law, a board may disseminate the minutes to the public marked if they are marked Draft or Tentative pending the board's final approval.

Such minutes need not contain any matter that is not required to be public.[33] The Freedom of Information Law authorizes a board to deny access to information in certain enumerated categories.[34]

In addition to the Open Meetings Law, the Freedom of Information Law contains what may be considered an "open vote" provision. The law requires that "a record of the final vote of each member" be compiled by the public body that identifies how individual members voted in every instance in which a vote was taken. Therefore, minutes that refer to a final vote must also specify who voted in favor of a motion and who voted against it.[35]

Usually minutes can be amended to clarify what actually happened at a particular meeting; but they may not be amended to reflect a change in mind, because such action could prejudice third parties who might have acted in reliance upon the original minutes. According to *Robert's Rules of Order*, if there is a change of mind, a motion to rescind or amend the action previously voted upon should follow.[36]

Publication

According to the provisions of the Education Law, "any school district board of trustees, board of education or other corporate body may publish the minutes of its proceedings "in the official newspaper or if no official newspaper has been designated, in any newspaper having general circulation in the school district."[37] However, there is no requirement that minutes be published.

6. Executive Sessions

An executive session is defined as "that portion of a meeting not open to the general public."[1] The word *portion* is significant here because it indicates, and courts have held, that an executive session must conducted *as part of* an open meeting and may *not* be considered a *separate* meeting. Therefore, a board must properly convene an open meeting *prior* to entering an executive session.

Topics that may be properly discussed in executive session and the procedures for entering into executive session are specifically prescribed by the law. In addition, because it is virtually impossible for any statute to cover every possible aspect of every situation, the courts have added their judicial interpretation to protect and promote the legislative intent of the law.[2]

Convening Procedures

The Open Meetings Law prescribes several procedural steps to which a public body must strictly adhere to before entering an executive session.[3]

First, a board member must make a motion during an open meeting to convene an executive session. In the absence of authorization given at an open meeting, a public body may not enter into an executive session.[4]

Second, the motion to convene must identify, with particularity, the general area or areas of the subject or subjects to be discussed.[5] In one case, a lower court held that a board's motion to convene for the stated purpose of "discussions regarding proposed, pending or current litigation" was insufficient to comply with the intent of the statute. In so holding, the court reasoned, "Executive sessions are mandated only in those limited circumstances enumerated in [section 105] of the Public Officers Law. These exceptions to the general rule must be narrowly scrutinized, lest the article's clear mandate be thwarted by thinly veiled references to the areas delineated thereunder. In order to be validly convened there must be strict adherence to the procedure set forth therein." The court further explained that "it is insufficient to merely regurgitate the statutory language; to wit, 'discussions regarding proposed, pending or current litigation.' This boilerplate recitation does not comply with the intent of the statute. To validly convene an executive session for discussion of proposed, pending or current litigation, the public body must identify with particularity, *the* pending, proposed or current litigation to be discussed during the executive session. Only through such an identification will the purposes of the Open Meetings Law be realized."[6]

Third, the motion to convene an executive session must be carried by a majority vote of the total membership of the board. For example, if a board has five members, and a majority of three is present at a meeting, a motion to enter into executive session would require all three votes; a two-to-one vote would not be sufficient.

Permissible Subjects for Executive Session

The Open Meetings Law enumerates and limits certain matters of public business that may be transacted by public bodies in executive sessions. These include

- Matters that will imperil the public safety if disclosed
- Any matter that may disclose the identity of a law enforcement agent or informer
- Information relating to current or future investigation of a criminal offense that would imperil effective law enforcement if disclosed
- Discussions about proposed, pending or current litigation
- Collective negotiations pursuant to Article 14 of the Civil Service Law
- The medical, financial, credit or employment history of a particular person or corporation, or matters leading to the appointment, employment, promotion, demotion, discipline, suspension, dismissal or removal of a particular person or corporation
- The preparation, grading or administration of examinations
- The proposed acquisition, sale or lease of real property or the proposed acquisition of securities, or sale or exchange of securities held by such public body, but only when publicity would substantially affect the value thereof[7]

We emphasize that the specific language of the law indicates a public body *may* enter into executive session; however, there is no requirement that a public body *must* confer in private, even though grounds for entering into executive session exist. Therefore, it appears a board may decide to discuss in a public meeting a matter that could be reserved appropriately for discussion in executive session. Nevertheless, as illustrated by the following judicial decisions, the propriety of a public body's decision to enter into executive session under one of the permissible subjects for discussion will be narrowly scrutinized by the courts.

Personnel Matters

Although the term *personnel* is not mentioned anywhere in the Open Meetings Law, it is the subject matter that has raised the most difficulty for boards entering executive sessions.[8] To ensure that matters of policy relating indirectly to personnel in general are discussed during open meetings, the law was amended in 1979 to enable a public body to enter into executive session to discuss personnel matters relating to a *particular* person or corporation. As such, executive sessions on personnel, for example, will be permitted only when the discussion concerns a "particular" person. This prevents a board from entering executive session on a general motion "to discuss personnel matters and negotiations" or "personnel layoffs."[9]

Matters involving tenured teachers also fall within this exception.[10] For example, voting to determine whether probable cause exists to bring 3020-a charges against a tenured teacher must be made by the board in executive session.[11]

Real Property

Another matter for discussion in executive sessions that has been the source of judicial debate involves the purchase and sale of real property. The Open Meetings Law, as amended, permits a public body to discuss "the proposed acquisition, sale or lease of real property or the proposed acquisition of securities, or sale or exchange of securities held by such public body" during an executive session, but "it must first be shown that publicity would substantially affect the value of the property."[12]

However, in another case a court refused to invalidate the sale of two schools negotiated in various executive sessions held by the board of education. Residents of the district had passed several referendums authorizing the board to sell the schools at various prices, but there were no buyers. Thereafter, the board continued to discuss several proposals for the purchase of the property. Most of the discussions were held in executive session "allegedly to protect the integrity of the offers and to secure for the people of the district the best possible financial return" for the property in question. A public hearing was scheduled and held to advise the community of the background of the proposed sale and the terms of the proposed contract. A board later passed a resolution authorizing the sale of the property. The petitioner challenged the sale by alleging the board violated various statutes, including the Open Meetings Law. The court, in reviewing the proceedings of the school board, determined, under the specific facts presented, the board of education did not violate the provisions of the Open Meetings Law.[13]

These cases emphasize that any determination regarding the propriety of a board's decision to hold an executive session pursuant to one of the enumerated exceptions will be highly dependent upon the attendant facts.

Proposed, Pending or Current Litigation

The Open Meetings Law also permits a public body to hold discussion regarding "proposed, pending or current litigation."[14] Courts have held that the stated purpose of this "exception" is "to enable a public body to discuss pending litigation privately, without baring its strategy to its adversary through mandatory public meetings."[15]

In one case, the Appellate Division held that a town board, which held an executive session based on the town attorney's belief that an adverse decision "would almost certainly lead to litigation," did not justify conducting the public business in an executive session. In so holding, the court reasoned that "to accept this argument would be to accept the view that any public body could bar the public from its meetings simply by expressing the fear that litigation may result from actions taken therein. Such a view would be contrary to both the letter and the spirit of the exception."[16]

Collective Bargaining Negotiations

The Open Meetings Law states a public body may conduct an executive session to discuss collective negotiations "pursuant to article fourteen of the civil service law" (more commonly known as the Taylor Law).[17] In one noteworthy case, a committee designated by a county legislative body sought to force a union to conduct collective bargaining negotiations in public. In that case, the Public Employment Relations Board (PERB) specifically ruled the Open Meetings Law does not apply to collective negotiations under the Taylor Law. In so ruling, PERB reasoned, "We have dealt with the question of whether the Open Meetings Law is applicable to collective negotiations under the Taylor Law . . . and held that it was not, saying 'collective negotiations sessions between a public body and an employee organization are by their nature not meetings within the contemplation of that law.'"[18] Therefore, such bargaining sessions need not be open to the public.

PERB added, "In the Taylor Law scheme, it is the chief executive officer who is statutorily charged with conducting negotiations on behalf of the employer. To the extent that the legislative body involves itself in collective negotiations, its actions are not authorized by, and may be violations of, the Taylor Law."[19] Because ratification of a tentative collective bargaining agreement does not appear to fall within the Open Meetings Law's limited exception for "collective bargaining negotiations," it seems that if a board, instead of the chief executive officer, has properly reserved the right to ratify the tentative agreement, such ratification vote should be taken in open session.[20]

PERB's decision was subsequently affirmed by the New York State Supreme Court. In short, PERB ruled that the Open Meetings Law does not apply to collective bargaining sessions. In other words, the Open Meetings Law, in light of the interpretation given the Taylor Law, would not give a school board member the inherent right to attend collective bargaining sessions.

On the other hand, a board's discussion of collective bargaining strategies, the status and progress of negotiations and other subjects relating to prospective or pending negotiations, are within the collective bargaining exception of the Open Meetings Law and may be discussed in executive session.

Mandatory Subjects for Executive Session

The Open Meetings Law provides, in effect, that when a matter may be *discussed* in executive session, it may also be acted *upon* in executive session. Boards of education, however, with certain limited exceptions, have long been required to take action on substantially *all* of their business during open meetings and not in executive session, pursuant to section 1708(3) of the Education Law.[21] Such exceptions include matters pertaining to the evaluation or placement of children with handicapping conditions and the voting of disciplinary charges against a tenured teacher under Education Law section 3020-a (2).[22] Section 3020-a hearings may be opened to the public at the option of the subject employee.[23]

Although the Education Law does not explicitly state that boards of education may not take action in executive session, the requirements of section 1708(3), as interpreted, have been deemed to override the more permissive requirements of the Open Meetings Law. Consequently, such judicial interpretations indicate that although boards of education may *discuss* in executive session the matters enumerated above, they may take *action* on such matters only during an open meeting.[24]

In addition, if a board intends to review a particular school employee's personnel records for one of the purposes enumerated in section 105 of the law, such records may be examined by a board only during an executive session, pursuant to part 84 of the commissioner's regulations. It is important to note, however, that this does not mean that all of the records that may be found in an employee's personnel file must be disclosed only in executive session; certainly some documents such as collective bargaining agreements and attendance records are appropriate for public disclosure.

The procedure by which board members may examine such records is relatively straightforward. Any board member may request the superintendent of schools to bring the personnel records of a designated employee or employees to an open meeting of the board. The board must then determine whether to conduct an executive session to examine the records. The superintendent must then present the designated records to the board during the executive session.

Information obtained from such records by board members may be used only to aid members in fulfilling their legal responsibilities in making decisions in matters of employee personnel, in developing and implementing personnel policies or such other uses that are necessary to enable the board to carry out its legal responsibilities. Employee personnel records must be returned in their entirety to the custody of the chief school officer at the conclusion of the executive session.[25]

Action Prohibited in Executive Session

A public body can never vote to appropriate public monies during an executive session. Therefore, any vote to spend public monies must be taken in public. For example, in one unreported decision a court held that personnel layoffs are primarily a budgetary matter and not among the specifically enumerated personnel subjects in section 105(1)(f) of the Open Meetings Law appropriate for discussion.[26]

Attendance

The Open Meetings Law permits attendance at an executive session by any member of the public body "and any other persons authorized by the public body."[27] Therefore, it seems clear that members of the staff of the public body and other parties whose advice or assistance the public body may wish to have may be permitted to attend an executive session.

In view of the fact that the law was amended to apply to committees of a public body, it seems apparent that a committee of a board of education may vote to conduct an executive session for a permitted purpose in the same manner as the full board.[28]

In addition, the New York State commissioner of education has ruled there is no time limit on the length of executive sessions other than that imposed by good judgment and the reasonable exercise of discretion.[29]

Minutes

As specified in chapter 5 ("Minutes," p. 26), because with few exceptions boards may not take action in executive session, minutes of an executive session need reflect only a record or summary of the final determination "of any action that is taken by formal vote."[30] Once again, the minutes of an executive session of a board of education need reflect only those matters where some "action" was properly taken (for example, the voting of charges against a tenured teacher). Therefore, if a board merely discusses a matter during executive session but takes no action, minutes of the executive session need not be compiled.

Again, minutes taken at executive sessions must be made available to the public *within one week* from the date of the executive session.[31]

7. Enforcing the Open Meetings Law

The Open Meetings Law provides that any "aggrieved" person can commence a proceeding pursuant to Article 78 of CPLR, requesting the court to compel a public body to perform a duty required by the law (mandamus) and/or declare that an action taken by the public body be invalidated and further prohibited (declaratory and injunctive relief).[1] A CPLR proceeding cannot be maintained to challenge any determination that can adequately be reviewed by some other body or officer.[2]

The Education Law provides that any person who feels aggrieved by any action taken by a school board may appeal such action to the commissioner of education.[3] The commissioner, however, has repeatedly held he has no authority to declare void any action taken in violation of the Open Meetings Law, and that the appropriate forum for addressing violations of the Law is in New York State Supreme Court by a CPLR article 78 proceeding.[4]

Whether to declare void any action taken by a public body in violation of the Open Meetings Law is a matter left to the court's discretion, to be exercised "upon good cause shown."[5] Thus, it is clear that not every violation of the Open Meetings Law triggers its enforcement sanctions.[6]

Mandamus

A CPLR Article 78 proceeding in the nature of mandamus is an appropriate remedy to compel the performance of a statutory duty that is ministerial in nature, such as a failure to comply with the Open Meetings Law.[7] In other words, if an individual believes a public body has failed to perform a duty required by the Open Meetings Law (for example, giving proper public notice of a meeting, publishing the minutes, etc.), he or she may bring a lawsuit requesting the court *to compel* the public body to perform the duty in question.

Declaratory Judgment and Injunctive Relief

The Open Meetings Law provides that any aggrieved person shall have the right to commence an action for declaratory judgment and injunctive relief. Thus, if an individual feels aggrieved by any action taken by a public body and wishes to have a court invalidate such action and prohibit the board from taking further similar action, he or she may bring a lawsuit requesting such (declaratory and injunctive) relief. However, where a public body's violation of the statute is found to have occurred in "good faith" or was otherwise "unintentional," the courts have sometimes refused to grant such relief.[8]

Invalidation of Action Taken

The Open Meetings Law provides that "an unintentional failure to fully comply with the notice provisions required by this article shall not alone be grounds for invalidating any action taken at a meeting of a public body."[9] Numerous courts have upheld this position.[10] Even where it is clear that a violation of the Open Meetings Law occurred, the petitioner must still make the required showing of "good cause" to be entitled to the "discretionary remedy" of invalidation.[11]

However, where the court finds the public body's failure to give proper notice was *not* "unintentional," any action taken at the improperly noticed meetings may be voided.[12] In one recent school case, the court found good cause had been shown to void action taken at an executive session where the notice of the meeting was found to be inadequate under the Open Meetings Law. The court reasoned that "[the board of trustees'] violations were not 'unintentional' . . . but calculated to minimize public awareness of [their] sensitive political decision to attempt settlement of a highly publicized matter. Such ongoing awareness is important in that it may well play a significant role in the degree of public concern about, and attendance at, future public sessions to approve a settlement. It may also influence the public's future choices in the board. The public's awareness . . . should be fostered through compliance with the Open Meetings Law."[13]

Such judicial decisions suggest that although the courts clearly have the discretion to nullify action taken by a public body in violation of the law upon good cause shown, they will often look carefully for signs of bad faith or an intentional violation before resorting to the more drastic remedy of declaratory and injunctive relief.

However, in another recent school case, a court invalidated actions taken by a school board where it found the board's repeated entries into executive session were "untenable" *despite the fact that the actions in question were taken in an open meeting.* The court refused to accept the board's argument that even if it was in violation of the Open Meetings Law, such violations were "cured" by the subsequent open meetings. The court reasoned that "although the Board and the Superintendent's efforts to inform parents, teachers and the public of the . . . School District's pending decision, were sincere and done in good faith, they cannot avoid the clear mandate of the Open Meetings Law."[14] Such judicial interpretation powerfully illustrates the courts' considerable discretion in enforcing violations of the Open Meetings Law.

"Curing" Unintentional Errors

In certain circumstances the courts have gone so far as to allow a subsequently held legal meeting at which the questioned action was taken to "cure" a prior violation of the Open Meetings Law.

In one noteworthy case, the state Supreme Court declared void an early version of a reapportionment plan because the meeting of the county legislature enacting it had violated the Open Meetings Law. The reapportionment plan was subsequently enacted at a public meeting after a public work session and public hearing were held. The petitioners claimed the prior illegal meeting "tainted" the subsequent legal meetings. Nevertheless, the Court of Appeals unanimously affirmed a decision of the Appellate Division that held "any violations of [the Open Meetings L]aw which led to the invalidation of the earlier version of the reapportionment plan were sufficiently *cured* by the two subsequent public meetings held by the county legislature" (emphasis added).[15]

In another case, a court ruled a school board's illegal advisory committee meetings, which were held in closed meetings with a majority of the full board present, did *not* taint the otherwise legal action of the public body (that is, the full board) to which it reported. The court held that even though such meetings were held in intentional violation of the Open Meetings Law, the board's action–ordering the closing of one of the district's schools–that was taken at an open meeting after a prior open hearing, sufficiently "cured" the prior illegality. In other words, because what was sought to be cured was only a report from an advisory committee that could make only a non-binding recommendation, and "because the petition failed to allege any violation of the Open Meetings Law at the meeting at which the action took place, the petition must be dismissed."[16]

Such judicial decisions illustrate the courts' inherent liberal discretion to deem a prior illegal meeting "cured" by a subsequent legal meeting at which the action in question was taken.

Costs and Attorneys' Fees

Under the Open Meetings Law, the court has the authority, in its discretion, to award costs and reasonable attorney's fees to the "successful party."[17] In other words, if a party brings an action alleging a violation of the Open Meetings Law and is victorious, a court *may*–but is not required to–reimburse the successful party for some or all of its expenditures incurred in bringing the action.[18] Further, in one case, a court refused a petitioner's request for attorney's fees as a "successful party," even where it found that a public body's failure to give notice was committed "intentionally."[19]

However, in one stinging decision, the Appellate Division found a county legislature's failure to adhere to previous court orders requiring compliance with the Open Meetings Law to constitute contempt of court, imposed a fine of $250 for its "persistent dereliction of the mandates of the [Open Meetings Law] statute" and awarded the successful party attorneys' fees.[20]

Statute of Limitations

The Open Meetings Law provides that "the statute of limitations in an article seventy-eight proceeding with respect to an action taken at executive session shall commence to run *from the date the minutes of such executive session have been made available to the public*"[21] (emphasis added). In other words, if a board is found to have violated the Open Meetings Law by improperly failing to publish the minutes of an executive session as required by the statute, a prospective petitioner will not be prevented from bringing a lawsuit until four months following the publication of the minutes have expired.[22]

Although not specified in the statute itself, judicial interpretation of the Open Meetings Law indicates that the four-month statute of limitations in a CPLR Article 78 proceeding runs from the date minutes were made available to the public regarding regular, special and other covered "meetings" as well.[23]

It is important for all public bodies to ensure compliance with the applicable notice and other procedural requirements of the Open Meetings Law to avoid numerous potential timely claims for "technical" and other unintentional violations of the statute.

PART 2

The Freedom
of Information Law

8. Introduction

New York State's Freedom of Information Law (FOIL) guarantees the public access to government records in order to encourage increased understanding of and participation in government.[1] The original FOIL, enacted in 1974, specified nine types of accessible records; all other records were excluded. The law was repealed and then reenacted effective January 1, 1978.[2] The current statute presumes access to *all records* unless the records fall within nine specified categories of exemptions. Consequently, the courts generally have construed FOIL liberally and its exemptions narrowly, requiring that "only where the material requested falls squarely within the ambit of one of the exemptions may disclosure be withheld."[3]

Definitions

In order to gain a better understanding of FOIL, it is important to have a grasp of the statute's basic terminology.

An *agency* is any state or municipal department, board, bureau, division, commission, committee, public authority, public corporation, council, office or other governmental entity performing a governmental or proprietary function for the state or any one or more municipalities thereof, except the judiciary or the state legislature.[4] Consequently, in the language of FOIL, school districts are agencies that must make their records available to the public. The New York State Supreme Court has held that a community college, for example, is an agency subject to FOIL.[5]

A *record* is any information kept, held, filed, produced or reproduced by, with or for an agency or the state legislature, in any physical form whatsoever, including but not limited to a report, statement, examination, memoranda, opinion, folder, file, book, manual, pamphlet, form, paper, design, drawing, map, photo, letter, microfilm, computer tape or disk, rule, regulation or code.[6]

In one New York State case, teaching and curricular materials used by a community college were records under FOIL and were not exempted from disclosure as "inter-agency or intra-agency materials."[7] Such judicial interpretation suggests that similar materials used by school districts may also be considered records that must be accessible to the public.

One New York State court has ruled that the notes made by the secretary to the New York State Board of Regents during the course of open and public meetings were official public records taken by the secretary in his official capacity and not a personal writing. Therefore, disclosure was required.[8] School boards should be aware that such reasoning may be applied to notes made by board members during open meetings.

School Districts' Responsibilities

School districts have several responsibilities under FOIL. They must have rules and regulations in place regarding these requirements. Such rules and regulations are usually kept in the form of a board of education policy and administrative regulation. Districts are required to adopt policies consistent with the law and the regulations promulgated by the Committee on Open Government[9] designating the time and place records are available for inspection, a records access officer and fees for copying records.[10]

The district must specify where and when records may be reviewed by the public. Generally, we recommend that districts provide interested parties with access to records at the main district office during regular office hours.

According to regulations of both the Committee on Open Government and of the commissioner of education, the district must appoint a records access officer who is responsible for handling public requests for records.[11] He or she must maintain an up-to-date list, called a *subject matter list*, of the categories of all records the district possesses *regardless* of whether or not the records are available to the public under FOIL.

The Appellate Division has held that agencies are required to provide the public with a reasonably detailed, current subject matter list; however, they are not required to further subdivide these subjects into subcategories.[12]

The district's records access officer must also assist the public in finding records and should either provide the records or deny access in a timely way. If records fall within the category of available records, the officer must make copies of the records or permit the person requesting the records to make copies. Also, upon request, he or she must certify that a copy is indeed a true copy of the original. If requested records are not in the district's possession, the officer must verify this fact. In addition, if the requested records are in the district's possession but cannot be located after a diligent search, it is the officer's responsibility to certify this as well.[13]

Under the Local Government Records Law, the superintendent, with the board's approval, must appoint a records management officer to ensure the orderly and efficient management of the district's records.[14] (For more information on records management, see chap. 13).

Under FOIL, the public may not be charged a fee for the inspection, verification or search for requested records. However, except where a different fee is prescribed by statute, the district may charge a fee not to exceed 25 cents per copy for photocopied records up to 9 by 14 inches or the actual cost of reproducing other types of records, excluding the fixed costs of the district, such as staff salaries. In the unlikely event the district has no photocopying equipment, members of the public may obtain a transcript of the requested records. In that case, the person requesting the transcript may be charged for the clerical staff time involved in its preparation.[15]

The district must give the public notice of the availability of its records. The regulations specify that the district conspicuously post and/or publish in a local newspaper the place where district records may be accessed; the name, title, business address and telephone number of the district's record's access officer; and the right to an appeal if access to records is denied, as well as the name and business address of the person designated by the district to hear such appeals.[16]

Generally, FOIL provides access to existing records. A school district need not create a record in response to a request. However, districts are required to compile and maintain certain types of records under FOIL. For example, the district must record the final vote of each board member of the district who votes at any board meeting. In addition, the district must maintain a record setting forth the name, office address, title and salary of every officer or employee of the district.[17]

9. Accessible Records

Under FOIL, all school district records are available for public inspection except those specifically defined in the statutory exemptions.[1] The courts have provided the forum for numerous challenges regarding the particular types of accessible records. These cases have clarified the types of district records that must be made available. Such judicial decisions illustrate the characteristics of records that may be exempt as well as those which are available.

It is important for school districts to realize that access to records cannot be limited to certain types or categories of people. In one case, a district tried to limit access to records to qualified voters only; however, the court held that under FOIL, *all persons* should have access to records, including citizens living outside the district. The court reasoned that "the Freedom of Information Law broadens the category of those to whom records are required to be made available beyond the disclosure required by section 2116 of the Education Law [which makes records available to qualified voters of the district]. Petitioner and her attorney, as well as other persons, *whether or not voters or in any way associated with the school district,* are intended to be benefited by [FOIL]"[2] (emphasis added).

Similarly, in another pivotal case, the state's highest court, the New York State Court of Appeals, determined that "the status or need of the person seeking access is generally of no consequence in construing FOIL and its exemptions."[3]

Although a district is required to provide access to records, there is no obligation to create records that are not already possessed or maintained by the district.[4] The courts have held that it is not the intent of FOIL to burden agencies with the expense and effort of preparing records for distribution to the public.[5] However, in one noteworthy case, the court determined that test scores listed alphabetically by student name should be made available. The court directed the district to scramble the listing and delete the students' names so they could not be identified. The court reasoned that such a requirement did not constitute the preparation of a new "record not possessed or maintained by the district."[6]

10. Exempt Records

FOIL specifies nine types of records that are exempt from disclosure to the public.[1] Nevertheless, the Court of Appeals has held that "while an agency is permitted to restrict access to those records falling within the statutory exemptions, the language of the exemption provision contains permissive rather than mandatory language, and it is within the agency's discretion to disclose such records, with or without identifying details, if it so chooses."[2] On the other hand, the same court has determined that an agency may not prescreen documents before permitting access to them.

In one case, the petitioner wanted access to the papers of the former mayor of Albany, Erastus Corning II. The court ruled that because the papers in question were being "held" or "kept" by a governmental entity that is an agency under FOIL, the records were available even though some of them were personal or unofficial in nature.[3] Although the agency had requested permission to screen the records in order to remove any materials of a personal nature, the court ruled that allowing an agency to unilaterally do so would thwart the purpose of the statute. The court reasoned that "the procedure permitting unreviewable prescreening of documents . . . could be used by an uncooperative and obdurate public official or agency to block an entirely legitimate FOIL request. There would be no way to prevent a custodian of records from removing a public record from FOIL's reach by simply labeling it 'purely private.'"[4]

Records Exempt by State or Federal Statute

The first exception to the right of access pertains to records that are specifically exempted from disclosure by state or federal statute.[5] In other words, to be exempted from disclosure by statute, an act of the state Legislature or Congress must indicate that particular records are outside the scope of public rights of access.

For example, in some instances, student records may be denied pursuant to the Federal Educational and Privacy Rights Act (FERPA), also known as the Buckley Amendment.[6] According to FERPA, information defined as directory information may be made available if the district has satisfied the statute's notice requirements.[7] These and related issues are more fully discussed in part 3.

In a recent case, the Appellate Division concurred with the State Education Department's Office of Professional Discipline in holding that information identifying a complainant's name, address and telephone number was properly denied because the Education Law makes such information confidential and not subject to disclosure except upon court order.[8] The court found that the Office of Professional Discipline's confidential investigatory files are exempt under FOIL and saw no justification for ordering their disclosure.[9]

Unwarranted Invasion of Privacy

The second exemption under FOIL provides that an agency may withhold records that, if released, would result in an unwarranted invasion of privacy.[10] Disclosures that would constitute an unwarranted invasion of privacy under FOIL include but are not limited to

- Disclosure of employment, medical or credit histories or personal references of applicants for employment
- Disclosure of items involving the medical or personal records of a client or patient in a medical facility
- Sale or release of lists of names and addresses if such lists would be used for commercial or fund-raising purposes
- Disclosure of information of a personal nature that would result in economic or personal hardship to the subject party, and such information is not relevant to the work of the agency maintaining it
- Disclosure of information of a personal nature reported in confidence to an agency and not relevant to the ordinary work of the agency[11]

According to FOIL, release of information will *not* be considered an unwarranted invasion of privacy if identifying details are deleted, the person to whom the record pertains consents in writing or the records sought pertain to the requesting individual and that person presents reasonable proof of identity.[12] Although cases involving personal privacy often require subjective judgments based upon the particular facts presented, the courts have provided considerable direction in this area.

Records Pertaining to Public Employees

Much of the case law concerning the privacy exemption involves records pertaining to public employees. For example, in various contexts it has been found that public employees enjoy a lesser degree of privacy than others, for they are required to be more accountable than others. Further, the courts have found that, as a general rule, records that are *relevant* to the performance of a public employee's official duties are available, for disclosure in such instances would result in a "permissible" rather than an "unwarranted" invasion of personal privacy.[13]

On the other hand, if records are *irrelevant* to the performance of one's official duties, they may be withheld or specific details may be deleted to protect against an unwarranted invasion of personal privacy. For example, while certain portions of a district employee's resume may be disclosable as relevant to the performance of his or her duties (for example, name or qualifications), other information contained in such a document would be irrelevant (such as home address, telephone number, Social Security number, etc.) and clearly deniable.[14]

Consistent with the view that records are available to the public unless they fit into one of these exempt categories, both the courts and the Committee on Open Government appear to search for creative ways to provide information as long as it is not burdensome to the district or other agency. For example, the Committee has advised that salary data for individual public employees is accessible. If the requester seeks a teacher's W-2 form, it could be provided as long as personal information other than the teacher's name and gross salary (such as payroll deductions) is deleted.

At least one court has upheld the right of access to information from teachers' personnel files. In the case, information regarding seven teachers was requested: the year each was hired; their present salary steps; and all written approvals for college courses, including the course name, credits earned and verification that these courses had been completed satisfactorily. The court ruled that educational transcripts are not to be made available because revealing personal information they may contain could constitute an unwarranted invasion of privacy.[15]

However, the court stated that some information extracted from these transcripts may be available. In addition, the court reasoned that "the information sought by petitioner is contained in summary forms prepared by the [board]. The fact that these summary forms are kept in the teachers' personnel folders, does not [by itself] make them exempt."[16] In so holding, the court determined there was no unwarranted invasion of privacy of the teachers involved and the information requested was accessible.

In another case, a court ruled that information gathered by the State Education Department detailing the dropout rates, placement rates, and factual field inspection reports from on-site inspections of licensed private schools and business schools was available. The court held that there was no evidence that this information was received confidentially or that releasing the records would constitute an unwarranted invasion of privacy. The court reasoned that the privacy exemption claim was unfounded because this was business or commercial information.[17]

Courts have permitted access to information such as city employee sick leave records, 3020-a settlement agreements, final determinations of guilt or misconduct and curricula vitae of all faculty at a particular college in several other cases, as long as irrelevant identifying details were deleted (for example, home address, Social Security number, etc.).[18]

It has been held in other circumstances that a promise or assertion of confidentiality cannot be upheld unless the statute *specifically confers* confidentiality. In one case, a state agency guaranteed confidentiality to school districts participating in a statewide survey on drug abuse. The court determined that the promise of confidentiality could not be upheld and the records were available because none of FOIL's enumerated grounds for denial could justifiably be maintained.[19]

In another recent case, the Appellate Division granted a university's request for access to police records regarding an investigation of a sexual assault that took place on the campus. The university wanted the records in order to defend against an anticipated lawsuit by the victim of the assault. The court ruled that the police department failed to establish that the records in question were exempt under FOIL.[20] The court determined that privacy of the witnesses was not an issue; because there was no proof that any of the witnesses had been promised anonymity, they were not confidential sources as defined by FOIL.[21] Therefore, there was no basis to deny access to the names and addresses of such witnesses.

Records of Charges against Tenured Teachers

It is noted that requests for records indicating charges pending against a tenured teacher may be withheld. The Education Law provides that hearings in such cases are private unless the teacher requests a public hearing.[22] In one case, where a member of the media wanted access to the name of the teacher and the charges in a disciplinary case involving a tenured teacher, the court ruled that such information was unavailable. Because the hearing was private, the court reasoned it was tantamount to an executive session. Consequently, by mandating privacy in disciplinary hearing procedures, the court upheld a denial of any records produced indicating the name of the teacher and the charges prior to any final determination.[23]

In denying access, the court stated that "in determining whether records are 'specifically exempted' by statute, the exemption must be clearly delineated and the statute narrowly construed. This does not mean, however, that the statutory language must contain a specific denial of disclosure; it is sufficient that the clear intent of the statute mandates confidentiality of the procedures or material."[24]

On the other hand, concurring with an advisory opinion from the Committee on Open Government, a lower court ruled that the media has a right to information about a disciplinary settlement agreement between a teacher and the district.[25] In that case, the teacher was brought up on tenured teacher disciplinary charges pursuant to section 3020-a of the Education Law and requested a public hearing.

After an initial hearing, a settlement was reached between the district and the teacher. A statement that identified the teacher by name and provided basic information about the settlement was issued to the press. It indicated that, as part of the disciplinary settlement, no further information would be provided to the media. The district claimed that further information was deniable pursuant to section 3020-a; however, the court found that section 3020-a did *not* prevent access, in part because the teacher had requested a public hearing.[26]

In an analogous situation, a public employee charged with misconduct engaged in a settlement agreement with a municipality. The parties to the settlement agreed that its terms would remain confidential. Notwithstanding the agreement of confidentiality, the lower court found that no grounds for denial existed to withhold the negotiated settlement. The court held that the records sought constituted the decision or final determination of the village and must be made available, even though arrived at by confidential settlement with the subject employee. In so holding, the court reasoned, "The citizen's right to know that public servants are held accountable when they abuse the public trust outweighs any advantage that would accrue to municipalities were they able to negotiate disciplinary matters with its employee with the power to suppress the terms of any settlement."[27]

These decisions illustrate that the courts may exercise considerable discretion in determining whether such information should be made available. In sum, although it is clear that the name of a tenured teacher and pending charges against him or her may be withheld prior to a final determination of guilt or misconduct, it is not altogether clear whether the terms of a settlement agreement between a teacher and a school district, even when reached pursuant to an agreement of confidentiality, are equally deniable. In fact, the Committee on Open Government has advised that the terms of such a settlement would result in a "permissible" rather than an "unwarranted" invasion of personal privacy, because "such a record is . . . relevant to the performance of the official duties of the School Board and the employee."[28]

Other Exemptions for Public Employees

The Court of Appeals has held that under FOIL, a non-profit organization that provides services to retired police officers is not entitled to the names and addresses of all retirees of the New York City Police Department who are currently receiving retirement benefits.[29] This case was decided after FOIL was amended in 1983 to include a section that *permits*, but does not require, an agency to disclose the home addresses of current public employees or officers or retirees from public employment.[30]

However, the sale or release of *lists* of names and addresses to be used for commercial or fund-raising purposes may be deniable under FOIL as an unwarranted invasion of privacy.[31] This is significant for school districts because they may receive such requests regarding lists of names and addresses they may possess, such as a list of participants in adult education courses.

In a recent case, a school board member sought information from the board of education regarding the names, home addresses, job titles and salaries of all district employees. The board claimed the member wanted access to personnel files; however, the court determined that the member was not requesting access to personnel files, and because the board made this information available to the general public, the board member could not be denied access. The board argued that the employees' home addresses should not be accessible. However, the court stated that although the district is not required to disclose the home addresses of its employees, it may disclose information that is exempt if it so chooses. Because the general public had access to this information, it could not deny access to one of its members.[32]

Impairment of Contract Awards or Negotiations

The third classification of documents that may be exempted under FOIL are records that, if disclosed, would impair present or imminent contract awards or collective bargaining negotiations.[33]

For example, in one case, the Appellate Division denied the requested disclosure of preliminary contract proposals and demands between the board and the teachers' association. The court based its decision on the affidavits of the district principal and the district's chief negotiator, which indicated the release of this preliminary information would seriously hinder ongoing collective bargaining negotiations.[34]

In contrast, in an especially noteworthy case, the president-elect of the School Administrators Association of New York State requested a copy of the report "Negotiations Information Services Salary Study for Administrators," which covered Suffolk County. This report was prepared by the local BOCES and was provided to member school districts on a subscription basis. The information requested consisted of data on teachers' and administrators' salaries and fringe benefits. Districts participating in the service could also request statistical information on other negotiations topics.

The Court of Appeals determined that just because this information was compiled by one agency for use by another, such information was not necessarily unavailable. The court stated that "though the burden is upon an agency claiming to be within one of the specific exceptions to [FOIL's] 'all records' requirements to demonstrate application of the exception, [BOCES] has made no effort in its papers to show that disclosure of the data requested would impair present or imminent collective bargaining within the meaning of [FOIL]." The court held that under FOIL the interagency material requested was available as "statistical or factual tabulations or data."[35]

Such judicial decisions are significant because they illustrate the courts' reluctance to prevent access to materials only tangentially related to contract awards or negotiations. To be successful, the agency must satisfy its burden by proving the "impairment" such disclosure would cause to "present or imminent" awards or negotiations.

Trade Secrets

Another set of records that may be exempted are those which can be classified as *trade secrets*, or information that, if released, would cause a substantial injury to the competitive position of the commercial enterprise.[36] This exemption rarely applies to school districts.

However, the application of this exemption was illustrated in one case where an insurance company had submitted computer programs and mathematical models and assumptions to the New York State Insurance Department at the department's request. The insurance company submitted the information with an application to use a certain method of computing dividends. The court ruled that the computer program and other information developed by the insurance company, which was not known by anyone else, was exempt from disclosure as a trade secret.[37]

The court reasoned that to rule otherwise would be unfair because competitors would have the unfair advantages of such available information without spending the time, energy or money to develop it on their own. Obviously, there would be a substantial injury to the insurance company's competitive position if this information were disclosed.[38]

Law Enforcement Information

The fifth exception in FOIL permits an agency to withhold records that are compiled for the purposes of law enforcement and that, if disclosed, would interfere with law enforcement investigations or judicial proceedings, deprive a person of the right to a fair trial or impartial adjudication, identify a confidential source or disclose confidential information relating to a criminal investigation or release criminal investigative techniques or procedures, except routine techniques and procedures.[39]

A unanimous Court of Appeals decision has held that certain portions of a special prosecutor's office manual illustrating confidential prosecution techniques were unavailable under this exemption.[40] In one noteworthy passage, the court reasoned that "however beneficial its thrust, the purpose of [FOIL] is not to enable persons to use agency records to frustrate pending or threatened investigations nor to use that information to construct a defense to impede a prosecution. . . . Disclosing to unscrupulous nursing home operators the path that an audit is likely to take and alerting them to items to which investigators are instructed to pay particular attention, does not encourage observance of the law. . . . The Freedom of Information Law was not enacted to furnish the safecracker with the combination to the safe."[41]

As with the trade secret exception, it is not likely that school districts would encounter requests that would fall under this provision, because school districts generally do not compile records for the purposes of law enforcement. Nevertheless, it is conceivable that a police department or a school district may attempt to use this exception upon receiving a request for records relating to incidents involving a search and seizure or an arrest made on a school district's property.

In contrast, in another case the Appellate Division unanimously denied a petitioner's request for access to records and physical evidence (such as tools and clothing) compiled during a criminal investigation that subsequently led to his conviction. The court determined that physical evidence does not fall within the definition of a record and thus is not subject to FOIL. The court also held that the names, addresses and statements of *confidential witnesses* compiled during criminal investigations are likewise exempt from disclosure under FOIL.[42]

Endangerment to the Safety of Persons

The sixth exception under FOIL permits an agency to withhold records that could endanger the life or safety of a person or persons if disclosed.[43]

For example, in one case, the Appellate Division ruled that unredacted copies of certain program and security assessment summaries of a correctional facility were deniable to an inmate.[44] While some of this information was deniable as interagency records, other information was denied because its release could pose a threat to the safety of some persons. The court determined that an agency does not have to prove that danger to a person's safety will *definitely* occur if the information is released; there need be only a *possibility* that the release of such information would endanger the lives or safety of persons.[45]

Interagency or Intra-Agency Materials

Another class of records that may be exempted under FOIL involves interagency or intra-agency materials.[46] *Interagency materials* are records transmitted *between or among* agencies (for example, correspondence between a school district and the State Education Department); *intra-agency materials* are those communicated *within* an agency (for example, a memo sent by the superintendent to the board of education).

This exemption permits an agency to withhold records identified as "inter-agency or intra-agency materials which are not: i. statistical or factual tabulations or data; ii. instructions to staff that affect the public; iii. final agency policy or determinations; or iv. external audits, including but not limited to audits performed by the comptroller and the federal government."[47]

The language quoted above is unusual because the statute states what cannot be withheld rather than what can be withheld. Although interagency and intra-agency materials may be withheld, they must be disclosed to the extent that they consist of statistical or factual tabulations or data, instructions to staff that affect the public, final agency policy or determinations or external audits.

Those materials may be withheld, however, insofar as they consist of advice, opinion, recommendations and the like. For example, in one case a court denied a school hockey official access to individual rating sheets prepared by coaches. The Office of Interscholastic Athletics implemented a rating system whereby coaches rated officials for each game they officiated. The court held that the rating sheets were "inter-agency documents" reflective of opinions, and that their dissemination would hinder an honest rating process that would be detrimental to the public interest.[48]

Statistical or Factual Tabulations or Data

Portions of interagency or intra-agency materials consisting of statistical or factual tabulations or data must be made available.

In one case, the Court of Appeals unanimously upheld lower court opinions in determining that the budget examiner's worksheets for the Cable Television Commission were discoverable as statistical or factual tabulations.[49] The Appellate Division had held that "it is only supporting statistical and factual tabulations which are discoverable. In the context of FOIL . . . use of the word 'statistical' or 'factual' does not exclude such information merely because an opinion is later based thereon."[50]

The court reasoned, "The mere fact that the document is a part of the 'deliberative' process is irrelevant . . . because [FOIL] clearly makes the back-up factual or statistical information to a final decision available to the public. This necessarily means that the deliberative process is to be a subject of examination although limited to tabulations. In particular, there is no statutory requirement that such data be limited to 'objective' information and there is no apparent necessity for such a limitation."[51] As such, statistical or factual information prepared in the process of developing a budget must generally be disclosed.

In another case, a district was required to release statistical information maintained by its board concerning certain incidents occurring in the New York City public school system.[52] The court upheld an advisory opinion of the Committee on Open Government, which stated that although the district must make the statistics available, it is not required to tabulate statistics or to prepare statistics on the requester's behalf. The committee's opinion also stated details that will identify particular students should be deleted and the remainder of the records be made available.[53]

Instructions to Staff That Affect the Public

Instructions to staff that affect the public are documents that are available under FOIL. In one case, a principal was not recommended for tenure. The superintendent then changed his recommendation based on a memorandum of understanding signed by himself and the principal. The media requested access to this memorandum, and access was denied by the district. The court ruled that the memorandum was available because it constituted instructions to the principal regarding his performance on the job. The court reasoned that because the principal interacts on a regular basis with teachers, the board of education and district students, his duties affect the public, thereby requiring that the document be accessible.[54]

Final Agency Policy or Determinations

In one noteworthy case, a unanimous Court of Appeals upheld the Appellate Division's ruling that had denied a New York City teacher access to documents prepared by a hearing panel that had heard her appeal of an unsatisfactory performance rating. On the basis of the documentation gathered by the panel, the chancellor of education had upheld the teacher's appeal, reversed the unsatisfactory rating and expunged it from her file. The teacher sought access to the panel's evaluations, recommendations and reasoning. The court determined that the panel's materials were not final agency determinations but were predecisional materials that had been prepared to assist in the chancellor's decision.[55]

The Appellate Division has also ruled that certain records concerning an investigation into a probation officer's performance were not available under FOIL. The court held that notes and communications made in preparation for the hearing and hearing transcripts were predecisional materials and were not reflective of final agency policy or determinations.[56] This case is relevant to school districts in instances involving public requests for information regarding employee disciplinary actions.

In a case involving a community college, the court held that the teaching materials used in a human sexuality course were available. The college had denied the request claiming the materials were not "agency records" under FOIL, and that they were exempt from disclosure pursuant to both FOIL (interagency or intra-agency materials) and "the constitutional principle of academic freedom." The court reasoned academic freedom was essentially irrelevant in this case because it has nothing to do with the public's right to access to information of governmental entities. In addition, the requested teaching materials that were authorized by the district could not possibly be "pre-decisional" or "deliberative" in nature because they had been in use for years and were considered college policy and determination and thus available records under FOIL.[57]

In another school case, when a father's request that his daughter be transferred to another school within a district was denied, he sought access to the records relating to the decision. The district denied access to the records. However, the court ruled that the intra-agency records in question, recommendations made by the superintendent that were adopted as the school board's rationale for its decision constituted the district's final determination and should be made available.[58]

In contrast, the Court of Appeals has ruled that a memorandum prepared for intra-agency use by the Metropolitan Transit Authority stating a position that *may* be taken in pending or prospective collective bargaining negotiations was deniable because it was not a "final determination."[59] School districts bargain collectively with their employees, so it is important for them to be aware of this case. Such judicial interpretation illustrates district records that state a position the district may take in ongoing or future negotiations may properly be withheld as intra-agency material and, potentially, on the grounds that disclosure would impair collective bargaining negotiations.

Information Prepared by Consultants

In one significant case, the Court of Appeals ruled the fact that an outside consultant had prepared the records for an agency had no bearing on whether or not the information was exempt under FOIL. The court determined that predecisional materials were not disclosable; however, statistical or factual tabulations should be redacted and made available regardless of the fact that the information was prepared by an outside consultant at the agency's request.[60] Therefore, if a school district has information prepared by a consultant, such information is treated no differently than other records prepared directly by the district. Consequently, unless this information falls within one of the statutory exemptions, it must be made available.

Examination Questions

The eighth classification of records that may be exempt under FOIL is examination questions or answers that are requested before the final administration of the questions.[61] This exemption is of particular relevance to school districts.

In one noteworthy case, the Appellate Division affirmed a lower court ruling holding that the decision as to when examination questions and answers have been finally administered is completely up to the agency (including a school district) administering the examination. In addition, the court ruled that the statute cannot be interpreted to mean that exam questions have been finally administered following their initial use, because agencies may reuse examination questions.[62] This decision appears to give districts considerable latitude in reusing exam questions and deciding when such questions are finally administered.

Computer Access Codes

The ninth FOIL exemption consists of records classified as computer access codes.[63] While cases covering this issue have not yet been decided by the courts, the Committee on Open Government has issued an advisory opinion regarding this exemption.[64] The committee advised that the numerical data encoded on the magnetic strips of Electronic Payment File Transfer Photo Identification Cards are not available records under FOIL. The magnetic strips contain numerical information that, when read by the computer, permits a cardholder on public assistance to receive benefits. According to the committee, the numerical data contains computer access codes that are exempt under the FOIL. The committee reasoned that keeping these codes secret is crucial because their release could lead to the improper issuance of public assistance benefits.[65]

Governmental/Executive Privilege

The principle of governmental privilege has, in the past, provided that an agency may withhold information if it is judicially determined that disclosure would, on balance, result in detriment to the public interest.[66]

In 1979, the principle was essentially abolished by a decision of the Court of Appeals. In apparently abolishing governmental privilege, the court stated that "the public policy concerning governmental disclosure is fixed by the Freedom of Information Law; the common-law interest privilege cannot protect from disclosure materials which that law requires to be disclosed. . . . Meeting the public's legitimate right of access to information concerning government is fulfillment of a governmental obligation, not the gift of, or waste of, public funds."[67]

In so holding, the state's highest court appears to have established that records may justifiably be withheld only pursuant to one or more of the grounds for denial specified in FOIL.

In another case, a public employee charged with misconduct reached a settlement agreement with a municipality. The parties to the settlement agreed that its terms would remain confidential. The union representing the public employee argued that the record should be protected from discovery by the common law privilege, in that "the harm apparent to the public interest if the negotiated settlement should be disclosed contrary to its express terms would be that it would seriously hamper the settlement of public sector labor disputes prior to arbitration."[68]

Notwithstanding the agreement of confidentiality, the court found that no ground for denial could justifiably be offered to withhold the negotiated settlement. In so holding, the court reasoned, "After some doubt as to whether the common law privilege remained intact after the passage of the Freedom of Information Law, it now appears settled by the Court of Appeals that the common law privilege has been pre-empted by the Freedom of Information Law. It is now incumbent on those opposing disclosure to identify the specific exemption under FOIL which excepts the subject records from disclosure."[69]

This judicial decision helpfully illustrates the application of FOIL's exemptions to agencies, such as school districts. In short, a school district cannot merely assert a ground for withholding information it does not wish to disclose; instead, the district must *prove* that the exemption from FOIL is applicable.

For example, a district preparing for, or in the midst of, contract awards or collective bargaining negotiations may successfully withhold certain records by asserting the exemption and proving the impairment to such activities a disclosure would engender.[70] In addition, a school district that is petitioned for access to its personnel records may seek to limit such access if such requests are proven an unwarranted invasion of the personal privacy of its employees or officials.[71]

Litigation

Is access to the records of a government agency under FOIL affected by pending or potential litigation between the person making the request and the agency?

The Court of Appeals has held that FOIL's mandate of open disclosure requires that an agency's public records remain as available to its litigation adversary as to any other person. While a suing party has no presumptive right under the CPLR to its adversary's files, the public has the right to inspect and copy the files of government under FOIL.[72]

The court rejected the agency's argument that the requested records were specifically exempted from disclosure by the CPLR. The CPLR demands that requested documents be "specifically designated," while FOIL requires only that the records be "reasonably described." The court found that the request for records upon the agency, while possibly insufficient under the CPLR, were sufficient under FOIL. The court reasoned, "We refuse to read into FOIL the restriction that, once litigation commences, a party forfeits the rights available to all other members of the public and is confined to [accessing records] in accordance with [the CPLR]."[73]

11. Procedures for Accessing Records

Time Limits

FOIL requires that within five business days of receiving a written request for a record reasonably described, the agency must make such records available to the person requesting it, deny such request in writing or furnish a written acknowledgment of the receipt of the request and a statement of the approximate date when the request will be granted or denied.[1]

In a recent decision, the Appellate Division upheld a lower court's ruling that a section of the New York City Board of Education's "Regulations Relating to the Inspection and Copying of Records" could not be amended to reflect the requirement contained in the regulation promulgated by the Committee on Open Government, which would require that the board either grant or deny access to records "within ten days" after acknowledgment of receipt of the request for records. The regulation was held to be invalid since it was inconsistent with FOIL, which contains no such time limitation but merely requires that the agency give the "approximate date" when such request will be granted or denied.[2]

Description of Records

FOIL requires that records requested of an agency must be "reasonably described" so that the agency may locate such records.[3]

Before the reenactment of FOIL in 1978, the Court of Appeals affirmed a lower court's ruling that a request for the budget examiner's files on the Cable Television Commission provided "sufficient information" to permit the agency to identify the requested records. The agency had denied a request for these records on the grounds of "vagueness of the request" and stated that the records requested were "not identifiable as a record." The lower court held that "it is not necessary that the party requesting the information identify it down to the last detail. . . . The responsibility of the person requesting the records is that he provide sufficient information to permit the agency to accomplish this duty. The budget examiner's files on the Cable Television Commission, even though it might consist of 40 individual folders as alleged by respondents, is sufficiently identifiable as to meet the requirements of the law."[4]

The Appellate Division has also held that if an agency has not compiled a list containing certain information requested of it, FOIL does not require that one be prepared by the agency.[5] In that case, the petitioner had requested a list containing the names of Monroe County employees whose positions had been terminated. The court found it "difficult to imagine that 276 jobs were eliminated and the employees notified of such termination without some record being kept of that transaction" and held that "if the county has never compiled a list of names of the eliminated employees, [FOIL] does not require that one be prepared. . . . Petitioner must, however, be granted access to those lists and documents which specifically identify the employees to be terminated and effectuate their removal."[6]

Such judicial reasoning suggests that a school district must grant access to other lists and documents that contain the same information that would have been set forth in the requested list, if it existed, unless such information is proven to be otherwise exempt.

12. The Appeal Process

Procedures

When a request for access to the records of an agency is denied, the requesting party has a right to appeal this determination. A common misconception has it that a person requesting school records under FOIL may appeal to the commissioner of education. The commissioner has reiterated that the appropriate forum for contesting alleged violations of FOIL is the New York State Supreme Court, not an appeal to the commissioner.[1]

The procedure for appealing denial of access to a record is prescribed by statute.[2] Within 30 days of denial of access to a record, the requesting party may appeal to the head, chief executive, governing body or designee of the agency in question. School districts, through adoption of rules and regulations, as described in "School Districts' Responsibilities" (p. 42), must designate an individual who is responsible for receiving and deciding appeals. Within 10 business days of receipt of the appeal, this individual must detail the reasons for further denial in writing or make the requested records available. Also, the school district must immediately send to the Committee on Open Government a copy of the appeal when the school district receives it as well as the agency's determination when it has been rendered.[3]

FOIL provides that any individual whose final appeal to an agency is denied may initiate a judicial review of this determination under Article 78 of the CPLR.[4] Also, case law has established that if an agency fails to respond to an appeal within the statutory time frame, the person requesting the record will then be entitled to seek a judicial remedy.[5] If access is denied pursuant to one of the statutory exemptions discussed earlier, the agency has the burden of proving that the record sought falls within one or more of these exemptions.[6] The Court of Appeals has reiterated this premise on numerous occasions.[7]

In addition, FOIL permits a court, in its discretion, to assess against the agency involved reasonable attorneys' fees and litigation costs incurred by a person who challenges a denial of access to records in court and substantially prevails. However, such fees and costs may be recovered only where the record in question is of "clearly significant interest to the general public" *and* "where the agency lacked a reasonable basis in law" for denying access to the record.[8] The courts have confirmed that the awarding of attorneys' fees can be left to their discretion. Such an award may not be disturbed unless there is shown to be an obvious abuse of the courts' discretionary powers.[9]

In addition to possible liability for attorneys' fees and litigation costs, under New York's Penal Law an agency that willfully conceals or destroys records with the intent of preventing the public from inspecting such records may be found guilty of a violation, punishable by up to 15 days in jail.[10]

Judicial Inspection of Records

In some instances, the courts may conduct an *in camera* (judicial) inspection of the records at issue in order to determine if they should be made available. In other words, the judge will review in chambers the actual records in dispute for the purpose of determining their availability or denial. However, courts have repeatedly stated that *in camera* inspection is not automatic and is not required in all cases. The agency involved should analyze the documents carefully to limit the need for *in camera* inspections, because a requirement that all such documents be judicially reviewed would be an unnecessary burden upon the courts.[11]

13. Management, Retention and Destruction of Records

The Local Government Records Access Law[1] and regulations of the commissioner of education require that every school district appoint a records management officer. This person's responsibilities include initiating, coordinating and promoting the systematic management of the district's records "in consultation and cooperation with other local officers."[2]

School districts also are required to review and adopt records retention and disposition schedules as established by the commissioner of education. The district's consent to use the schedule continue until the district rescinds its authorizing resolution, the commissioner's consent is withdrawn or the schedule is superseded and replaced by the commissioner.[3] Records not on the schedule may not be disposed of without the consent of the commissioner.[4] To dispose of records legally, the district clerk must apply to do so after an official resolution has been passed by the board. The application must certify the records no longer need to be preserved because they have no more administrative, legal or fiscal value.[5]

School districts and other local governments may apply for grants to help finance the costs involved in records management. For more information on these grants and for other information on records management and retention, contact the State Education Department, State Archives and Records Administration, Albany, New York 12230. For more information regarding the destruction of student records, see part 3.

PART 3

The Family Educational Rights and Privacy Act

14. Introduction

In 1974, Sen. James L. Buckley of New York State proposed and the federal government enacted the Family Educational Rights and Privacy Act, commonly known as either the Buckley Amendment or FERPA.[1] The act was designed to preserve the confidentiality of student records by ensuring that no part of a student's record be divulged to any person, organization or agency (other than designated school staff) without written consent from the parent or "eligible" student. The request must describe the specific information to be divulged, the purpose of the disclosure and the entity to whom disclosure is to be made, except under certain enumerated conditions. The act allows parents and eligible students to inspect such records and challenge the content to ensure the records are not inaccurate or misleading; it also provides parents and eligible students with notification of these rights and protections.

While New York's Freedom of Information Law (FOIL) governs access to records in possession of all local governments, including school districts and BOCES, rights of access to student records are governed by FERPA and its implementing regulations.

Compliance with FERPA

The U. S. Department of Education is responsible for "investigating, processing, reviewing and adjudicating violations" of the act and for handling complaints about alleged violations.[2] Because much of the information concerning the department's interpretation of FERPA is available from the implementing regulations it has promulgated, most of the following discussion relates to these regulations.[3] To receive more information, write to the Family Policy Compliance Office, U. S. Department of Education, Room 3017, FB-6, 400 Maryland Avenue, S. W., Washington, D. C. 20202-4605.

15. Rights of Parents and Eligible Students

Definitions

FERPA is designed primarily to protect the rights of parents of students and eligible students. An *eligible student* is one who has reached 18 years of age or is attending an institution of postsecondary education. Such a student receives all of the rights accorded to and consent required of parents under FERPA and related regulations. In addition, neither the act nor the regulations prevent school districts from giving students rights beyond those given to parents.[1]

There are numerous aspects to the rights provided by FERPA to parents and eligible students. The act and its regulations require federal funds to be withheld from any "educational agency or institution" that permits disclosure of education records or personally identifiable information contained in such records other than directory information to any individual, agency or organization, except certain defined individuals, without the written consent of the parent or eligible student.[2]

For our purposes, we shall consider an *educational agency or institution* to be a school district or BOCES. In the majority of cases, school districts and BOCES in New York State are subject to the act and its regulations.[3]

In the context of the act, *disclosure* means to permit access to or to release, transfer, or otherwise communicate the contents of education records or the personally identifiable information contained in those records to any party by any means, including oral, written or electronic means.[4]

Records

To understand what is permitted, required and prohibited under FERPA and its regulations, one must understand the different types of records that are subject to the act.

Records are any information recorded in any way, including but not limited to handwriting, print, tape, film, microfilm and microfiche.[5]

Education records are records, files, documents and other materials that contain information directly related to a student and are maintained by an educational agency or institution or by a person acting for such agency or institution.[6]

Education records do *not* include records of instructional, supervisory and administrative personnel and educational personnel who work with them that are in the sole possession of the maker of the records and are not accessible or revealed to any other person except a substitute.[7] These records include informal notes or "memory joggers" about a student made by a teacher. To be exempt, they may not be shared with anyone except a substitute filling in for that teacher. This exemption "is strictly construed[;] notes lose their exempt status if they are shown to any person, including the student."[8]

Nor do education records include records of a law enforcement unit of an educational agency or institution, but only if education records maintained by the agency or institution are not disclosed to the unit, and the law enforcement records are maintained separately from education records, maintained solely for law enforcement purposes and disclosed only to law enforcement officials of the same jurisdiction.[9]

Records maintained in the normal course of business related to someone employed by an educational agency or institution exclusively in his or her capacity as an employee but who is not in attendance there are not education records.[10]

In one case, a public school teacher argued that FERPA prevented her school district from releasing her college transcript as an "education record" in response to a request under her state's open meetings law. The federal court dismissed the argument because the teacher was not "in attendance" at the school as required under FERPA and because the teacher's college transcript, although it was on file with the district, was not "made and maintained" by the district.[11] Thus, the disclosure of this transcript was not subject to FERPA's requirements.

In contrast, records kept on a *student* who is attending an educational institution or agency and is employed as a result of his or her student status are education records and are not exempted from FERPA requirements.[12]

Records of a student 18 years of age or older who attends an institution of postsecondary education that are made or maintained by a physician, psychiatrist, psychologist, or other recognized professional or paraprofessional acting in his professional or paraprofessional capacity, or assisting in that capacity, and are made, maintained or used only in connection with the provision of treatment to the student and are not available to anyone other than persons providing such treatment or a physician or other appropriate professional of the student's choice are not education records.[13]

Records that contain only information about an individual after the person is no longer a student at that agency or institution are not education records.[14]

In part because FERPA is a federal statute, New York State's Committee on Open Government has no formal role in its interpretation. However, because sometimes FERPA regulations are implied in interpretation of the Freedom of Information Law, the committee occasionally comments and/or consults with the Department of Education on the act.

One of the committee's advisory opinions was concerned with whether "copies of all investigations, decisions, reprimands, etc. (if any) in the employment or personnel file of [a] teacher" concerning an incident involving a student, were disclosable to the parent of the student.[15]

After considering the issues related to FOIL concerned in the request, the committee's advisory opinion analyzed the implications of FERPA. The key issue was whether the materials sought constituted "education records." The Department of Education advised that "the documentation in question, if it is 'directly related to a student,' is an 'education record' that should be disclosed to the parent of the student."[16]

An evaluation in the teacher's file that was related to the incident apparently played a role in the committee's analysis. According to the opinion, if "the evaluation was 'made and maintained in the normal course of business,' as is likely the case with respect to routine evaluations of all teachers, it would not be an 'education record' subject" to FERPA. In such a case, rights of access would be determined solely under FOIL. If, however, the evaluation was prepared as a result of the incident and related directly to the student, the department would consider it a disclosable "education record."[17]

The committee also noted that section 89(6) of FOIL states, "Nothing in this article shall be construed to limit or abridge any otherwise available right of access at law or in equity of any party to records." Thus, if the record were accessible to the parent under FERPA, "nothing in FOIL . . . could be asserted to withhold the record."[18]

Directory information relating to a student includes but is not limited to the student's name, address, telephone listing, date and place of birth, major field of study, participation in officially recognized activities and sports, weight and height of members of athletic teams, dates of attendance, degrees and awards received, and the most recent previous educational agency or institution attended by the student.[19] Directory information is discussed more fully in "Directory Information" on page 77.

Release of Records with Consent

Except for the cases of individuals discussed under "Release of Records without Consent" (p. 74), a school district must obtain a signed and dated written consent of a parent or eligible student before it discloses personally identifiable information from the student's education records.[20]

The regulations require that the written consent specify the records that may be disclosed, state the purpose of the disclosure and identify the "party or class of parties to whom the disclosure may be made." When a disclosure is made under this part of the regulations, the district must provide a copy of the disclosed record should the parent or eligible student request it. In addition to this, when a disclosure is made in this manner, the district must provide a copy of the disclosed record to the student if the parent of a non-eligible student requests it.[21]

Release of Records without Consent

There are individuals to whom education records *may* be released *without* the prior consent of the parent or eligible student. These are other school officials and teachers within the school district determined by the district to have legitimate educational interests. This is interpreted by the U. S. Department of Education as those school employees "who have a need-to-know."[22]

A memorandum to school superintendents from the State Education Department in 1983 discussed the responsibility of school districts to share information on individual students with handicapping conditions with what was then SED's Office of Vocational Rehabilitation (now the Office of Vocational and Educational Services for Individuals with Disabilities). According to the memo, in such cases FERPA's requirements must be satisfied and, therefore, "where educational records containing assessment, classification, educational progress, vocational training and other information on an individual handicapped student are to be shared with a vocational rehabilitation counselor the school district would obtain prior consent of the parent for such disclosure," thus implying the record would *not* be released without consent.[23]

Officials of other schools at which a student seeks to enroll may review records without prior consent. However, the regulations require the school district disclosing the information to make a "reasonable attempt" to notify the parent or eligible student at his or her last-known address, unless the parent or student had initiated the disclosure or the school district's policies include a notice that it forwards education records to institutions in which the student intends to enroll that have requested the records.[24]

Upon the request of the parent or eligible student, the school district must provide a copy of the disclosed record and give the parent or eligible student an opportunity for a hearing if either one should request amendment of the records (see chap. 15).[25]

A school district also may disclose an education record to another institution if the student concerned is enrolled in or receiving its services. The district still must fulfill the requirements for other disclosures.[26]

Authorized representatives of the U.S. comptroller general, the U. S. secretary of education or state and local educational authorities do not need prior consent to review records.[27]

In one New York State case involving a dispute regarding officials permitted such information, a judge strictly construed this provision, holding that the state comptroller was not entitled to a computerized list of students who had been identified as candidates for a dropout program.

The judge reasoned that the comptroller was not an educational official and thus was not entitled to the records.[28] In so holding, the court stated, "The [board of education] suggested reasonable alternatives to providing the [state comptroller] with the information sought, and though the [comptroller] claims the methods suggested would compromise the integrity of the audit, it would appear Congress has decided that the need for confidentiality outweighs other considerations."[29]

Such judicial interpretation illustrates that certain conditions apply to disclosure even for those officials permitted access. Such access appears limited to situations evidencing a *specific need* for education records in connection with an audit or evaluation of any federally or state-supported education programs or for the enforcement of or compliance with federal legal requirements that relate to these programs.[30]

Except when collection of personally identifiable data is specifically authorized by federal law, or when the parent or eligible student has given written consent to the disclosure, any data collected by such officials must be "protected in a manner which will not permit personal identification of individuals except the officials" referred to above. For example, the information collected must be destroyed when no longer needed for the audit, evaluation of programs and enforcement of federal legal requirements.[31]

Records may be reviewed without prior consent in connection with a student's application for or receipt of financial aid if the information they contain is necessary to determine eligibility for, the amount of or conditions for receiving the aid, or to enforce the terms and conditions of the aid.[32]

Records may be reviewed without prior consent by state and local officials to whom such information is specifically required to be reported or disclosed pursuant to state statute adopted prior to November 19, 1974.[33]

Organizations conducting studies on behalf of educational agencies or institutions (including school districts) for the purpose of developing, validating or administering predictive tests; administering student aid programs; or improving instruction may review records without prior consent. However, a school district may disclose information to these organizations only if the studies are conducted in a manner that will not permit the identification of students and their parents by persons other than the organization's representatives and if the information will be destroyed when it is no longer needed for the study.[34]

Accrediting organizations that must carry out their accrediting functions may review records without prior consent.[35]

Parents of a dependent student who are defined as such in the Internal Revenue Code may review records without prior consent.[36]

Individuals entitled to the information because of judicial order or lawfully issued subpoena may review records without prior consent. In these situations the school district may disclose the information only if the district makes a "reasonable effort to notify the parent or eligible student of the order or subpoena in advance of compliance."[37]

"Appropriate parties" in connection with an emergency may receive records without prior consent if knowledge of the information is necessary to protect the health or safety of the student or other individuals.[38] The regulations in this area are to be "strictly construed" according to the regulations.[39]

One issue related to health and safety that would most likely be classified under this category is information about suspected child abuse. New York State Education Law requires school districts to develop and maintain written policies and procedures on reporting child abuse pursuant to the Social Services Law and Family Court Act.[40] Mandatory reporting of child abuse or neglect and reporting procedures must be included in the schools' policies and procedures.[41] The Social Services Law provides immunity from liability for school officials making reports in good faith.[42]

Section 3028-a of the Education Law provides immunity from liability to certain school personnel "having reasonable cause to suspect that a secondary or elementary student under twenty-one years of age is a substance or alcohol abuser or substance dependent . . . report such information to the appropriate . . . school officials pursuant to the school's drug policy or if the school has no drug policy to the school's principal or the parents or legal guardians of such student."[43]

Education records do not include "treatment records" for students 18 years of age or older (or those attending a postsecondary school), so these need not be made available to a parent or eligible student. The student may, however, have those records reviewed by a physician or other appropriate professional of his or her choice.[44]

School health records of a student of less than 18 years of age are more accessible, especially to his or her parent. One article addressing this issue noted,

> The Buckley Amendment, while intended to protect the privacy of the individual student and his or her family, may, to some extent, have the opposite effect when applied to health and medical records in schools, particularly given the nature of today's health services. Not only are school health records accessible to parents without review for minors' rights to privacy around protected medical issues, but they may also be accessible to other school staff members who may have no compelling need to know confidential health information which a student shares with the school nurse, or who may not have adequate knowledge of the health sciences to understand, interpret and utilize such health information appropriately.[45]

In addition, several other issues regarding the release of student health records have arisen. For example, the Alcohol, Drug Abuse and Mental Health Administration and the Family Policy Compliance Office of the Department of Education (the agency charged with interpreting and enforcing FERPA) were asked how FERPA relates to the Alcohol and Drug Abuse confidentiality statutes in regard to the records of a school-based Student Assistance Program (SAP).[46] FERPA's regulations permit a parent to inspect and review his or her child's education record, while the regulations under the confidentiality statutes prohibit the disclosure of alcohol and drug treatment records except with the consent of the student or patient or in other specific instances.

A joint opinion of the two agencies apparently determined that releasing the information covered by the confidentiality regulations to the student's parent requires the student's consent. To release it to third parties, "consent must be obtained from *both* the minor (to satisfy the confidentiality regulations) and the parent (to satisfy the FERPA regulations)" (emphasis added). According to the agencies, this interpretation, which reads the FERPA consent requirement into the confidentiality regulations, "reduces the potential for conflict" between the two sets of regulations. Other provisions of the regulations also allow for consistent interpretation and further reduce the conflict, such as, under the confidentiality regulations, the ability of "any person having a legally recognizable interest in disclosure to apply for a judicial order authorizing disclosure for purposes other than criminal investigation or prosecution, which would typically include compliance with FERPA."[47]

Another noteworthy health-related statute applicable to New York State school districts is Article 27-F of the Public Health Law, which restricts the disclosure of confidential information about AIDS or HIV related to individuals, including students. For the most part, disclosure is contingent upon a New York State Department of Health authorization for release form signed by the individual or person authorized by law to consent on behalf of the individual, if such person lacks the "capacity to consent" as defined by the law; or the issuance of a court order requiring the release of such information. School districts should be very careful before releasing any type of medical records, but especially those regarding AIDS or HIV, because the statute carries stiff penalties.[48]

Individuals may review records without prior consent when their information has been designated as "directory information" by the school district.[49]

Directory Information

One of the keys to understanding FERPA and its regulations is understanding the concept of "directory information." This type of data includes personal information about individual students. Directory information *may* be disclosed if a district has given public notice to parents of its students before disclosing the information. Notice *must* include the types of personally identifiable information that the district has designated as directory information. Personally identifiable information is defined under the regulations as including but not being limited to the student's name; the student's parents' name or other family member's name; the address of the student or student's family; and any personal identifier such as the student's Social Security number, personal characteristics or other information that would make the student's identity easily traceable.[50]

The designation (or non-designation) of such information is very important. In one New York State case, decided in 1983, an individual requested a community college to provide the names and addresses of all students who are or would be enrolled in the fall semester. The college refused to fulfill the request, and the matter went to court. The court ruled for the college on two grounds: first, the college had chosen not to include students' names and addresses in its classification of directory information; and, second, the petitioner had not demonstrated a need for the information that outweighed the students' right to privacy. Had the petitioner done so, the court could have permitted disclosure by court order.[51]

Names and addresses of students can be personally identifiable information that cannot be disclosed without consent *and* directory information that can be released pursuant to its designation as such following the notice requirements discussed in this section. For example, if a school board member desired access to the names and addresses of students' parents to assist in his or her campaign for reelection to a board, such personally identifiable information would not be disclosable without compliance with FERPA's notice requirements.

In one case, a court determined that where only names and addresses and no other personally identifiable information were to be released, and the institution had published a notice that complied with the FERPA regulations' requirements, no written consent was necessary.[52]

Also, it should be noted that military recruiters have no inherent right to directory information in the absence of proper public notice to parents and students. During the Persian Gulf war of 1991, some school districts voted to change their policies on requests for directory information. The Los Angeles Board of Education voted to stop honoring any requests for directory information about its students, whether requested by the military or private marketers. In San Francisco, the board voted unanimously to prohibit the release of directory information to military recruiters without the specific written consent of a student's parents.[53]

Such action illustrates that although FERPA is designed to protect a student's right to privacy, school boards still maintain considerable local control over what may or may not be released.

Notice must include a parent's or eligible student's right to refuse to let the district designate any or all of those types of information about the student as directory information and the period of time within which a parent or eligible student can notify the district in writing that he or she does not want any or all of those types of information about the student designated as directory information.[54]

Both the regulations and the case law indicate that a school district may, however, disclose directory information about former students without meeting the conditions described above.[55] The district may also disclose directory information to a parent of a student who is not an eligible student or to the student himself or herself.

The regulation neither forbids nor requires a school district to disclose personally identifiable information from the education records of a student to any of the parties noted above.[56] Therefore, it is important that the board use its discretion and carefully consider the available alternatives in developing its policy on release of student records.

There are at least two New York State cases that concern the important issue of the release of information on student records without prior consent of those involved.

In *Matter of Kryston v. Board of Education*, a parent of a student sought disclosure of certain standardized reading and mathematics test scores of 75 children who attended third grade in one of the district's schools during the 1977-78 school year. Although the requesting party sued for the release of the information under FOIL, there were also implications related to FERPA in the appellate court decision. The court held that the release of the test scores in alphabetical order of the students' names would violate their personal privacy, but the order of names could be scrambled in other than alphabetical order so that the students' scores would not be personally identifiable. As such, the scores had to be disclosed.[57]

The court also made it clear that such scrambling of the scores and names did not amount to the preparation of a new record, an action that is specifically not required under FOIL. The court further reasoned that even if there was doubt on that issue, "it would properly be resolved in favor of the [requesting party] since public disclosure statutes, both State and Federal, have been liberally construed to permit maximum access to documents."[58]

Would the same hold true with a request for the school records of a smaller number of students?

This issue was addressed in another New York State case, where a teacher sued the board of education, two students and their parents to recover damages for injuries allegedly sustained when the students attacked him in the classroom. The teacher attempted to compel the district to produce medical and personal records of the students. The city, representing the district, opposed the request solely on the grounds that FERPA requires denial of the request.[59]

The justice stated that because this was a "highly unusual" case, with a request for the records of only two students rather than those of large numbers of pupils, the court's "first concern is to insure that the students involved have an opportunity to contest the release of the records." The judge held that the students had to have an opportunity to be heard before the court ordered the release of the information. He further determined that the burden of giving notice of the opportunity rested on the requesting party rather than on the district, where FERPA places it, because, the justice believed, "in this atypical case . . . the party seeking disclosure should properly be responsible for providing notice. In the court's view, such notice will satisfy [FERPA] and the HEW [now Department of Education] guidelines . . . regardless of its source." The court also stated nothing would preclude the school, at its discretion, from giving additional notice to the students affected.[60]

"Redisclosure" of Information

A school district may disclose only personally identifiable information from an education record on the condition that "the party to whom the information is disclosed will not disclose the information to any other party without the prior consent of the parent or eligible student." The officers, employees or agents of a party who receive information in this manner may use it only for the purposes for which the disclosure was made.[61]

However, the regulations do not prevent a school district from disclosing personally identifiable information with the "understanding that the party receiving the information may make further disclosures of the information" on behalf of the district if the disclosures occur under conditions where prior consent to disclose is not required, the district has complied with record-keeping requirements and the district informs the party to whom disclosure is made of the above requirements.[62]

Once again, these requirements do not apply to disclosures of directory information to the parent of a student who is not an eligible student or to the student.[63]

Inspection and Review

Parents and eligible students have the right to inspect and review all of a student's education records maintained by a school. The school district must comply with a request for access to records within "a reasonable period of time, but in no case more than 45 days after it has received the request."[64]

FERPA regulations require only that the district respond to reasonable requests for explanations and interpretations of the records.[65] It should be noted, however, that under FOIL, districts must, within five days of receipt of a request for a record, make the record available, deny access in writing (giving the reasons for denial) or furnish a written acknowledgement of receipt of the request and a statement of the approximate date when the request will be granted or denied.[66]

Another contradiction between New York State law and FERPA concerns whether schools must provide copies of education records. The Department of Education has stated FERPA does not require school districts to provide parents with copies of records unless "the distance is great enough to make it impractical for the parent to visit the school to review the record." In such cases, the school must make copies of the records and send them to the parent upon request.[67]

However, FOIL requires that, upon request, accessible records be copied; thus, a parent or eligible student requesting a copy of an education record *would* be entitled to it.[68]

Nevertheless, fees may be charged for any record made, pursuant to both FERPA's regulations (unless the imposition of a fee "effectively prevents a parent or eligible student from exercising the right to inspect and review the student's records") and FOIL.[69]

There is one noteworthy limitation on the right to inspect and review records for public school students and their parents: if the education records of a student contain information on more than one student, the parent (or eligible student) may inspect, review or be informed of only the specific information about his or her child.[70]

Request for Amendment of Records

Parents and eligible students have the right to request a school district to correct records believed to be "inaccurate, misleading, or in violation of the student's rights of privacy or other rights."[71]

After the request has been made, the school district must decide whether to amend the record as requested within a "reasonable time" after receiving the request. Should the district decide not to amend the record as requested, it must inform the parent or eligible student of its decision and of the requesting party's right to a hearing.[72]

If both parties agree that an explanatory note alone is the appropriate remedy, such a note can be included in the record. To require a hearing under such circumstances would be "burdensome" and unnecessary, according to the secretary of education. However, if one or the other of the two parties should disagree, the parents or eligible student must exhaust the remedy afforded by the hearing process *before* entering an explanation in the record.[73]

Hearings

School districts are required to give a parent or eligible student an opportunity for a hearing when the contents of the student's education records are challenged on any of the grounds described above.[74]

The hearing must meet the following *minimum* requirements:

- The school district must hold the hearing within "a reasonable time" after it has received the request for a hearing from the parent or eligible student.[75]
- The school district must give the parent or eligible student notice of the date, time and place, "reasonably in advance of the hearing."[76]
- The hearing may be conducted by any individual, including

a school district official, who does not have a direct interest in its outcome.[77]

- The school district must give the parent or eligible student a "full and fair opportunity to present evidence relevant to the issues raised. The parent or eligible student may "at their [*sic*] own expense, be assisted or represented by one or more individuals of his or her own choice, including an attorney.[78]

- The school district must make its decision "in writing within a reasonable period of time after the hearing."[79]

- The decision must be based "solely on the evidence resented at the hearing and must include a summary of the evidence and the reasons for the decision."[80]

If, as a result of the hearing, the district decides that the information *is* "inaccurate, misleading or otherwise in violation of the privacy or other rights of the student," it must amend the record accordingly and inform the parent or eligible student of the amendment in writing. If the district decides that the information *is not* "inaccurate, misleading or otherwise in violation of the privacy or other rights of the student," it must inform the parent or eligible student of the right to place a statement in the record commenting on the contested information in the record or stating why he or she disagrees with the district's decision, or both.[81]

If a statement is placed in the education records of the student, the district must maintain the statement with the contested part of the record for as long as the record is maintained and disclose the statement whenever it discloses the portion of the record to which the statement relates.[82]

Rights of Non-custodial Parents

The regulations define a parent of a student and includes a natural parent, a guardian or an individual acting as a parent in the absence of a parent or guardian. But what are the rights of a non-custodial parent?

The implementing regulations indicate that "either parent" must be given full rights under the act by the school district, unless the district has been provided with evidence that there is a "court order, state statute, or legally binding document relating to such matters as divorce, separation, or custody that specifically revokes these rights."[83]

The Department of Education has explained that "in the case of divorce or separation, a school district must provide access to both natural parents, custodial *and* noncustodial, unless there is a legally binding document that specifically removes that parent's FERPA rights. In this context, a legally binding document is a court order or other legal paper that prohibits access to education records, or removes the parent's rights to have knowledge about his or her child's education."[84]

The department has also noted that FERPA simply establishes parents' right of access to and control over education records related to the child; custody or other residential arrangements for the child do not affect these rights. Because rights under FERPA are given to both parents, the parent with custody cannot prevent the non-custodial parent from exercising them unless there is a court order or other binding instrument prohibiting access. Accordingly, the school district does not need the permission of the custodial parent to give access to the non-custodial parent. And, as found by a New York State court, where there is a separation agreement but no divorce or court order affecting custody, visitation or support, the custodial parent has no right to deny the non- custodial parent his or her rights under FERPA.[85] Also, FERPA does not require schools to keep parents informed of a child's progress, whether or not his or her parents are divorced.

Another question answered by the department is whether FERPA requires that the non-custodial parent be informed of and have the right to attend teacher conferences. Because FERPA does not address conferences for the purpose of discussing student progress, the department has stated that schools have no obligation under FERPA to arrange such conferences; however, "if the records of conferences are maintained, the non-custodial parent has the right to see those records."[86]

Further, the act does not require that the non-custodial parent receive general notices, such as lunch menus, PTA information, announcement of school pictures and other such information, because these are not "education records" as defined by FERPA. Accordingly, the department has stated that school districts will be in compliance with the act as long as the custodial parent receives notification.[87]

Rights of Joint Custodial Parents

What about a situation where the parents are separated or divorced or are otherwise living apart but have joint custody of their child or children?

This issue was addressed by the U.S. Court of Appeals for the Second Circuit, which has jurisdiction over New York State. In one important New York State case, a father shared joint custody of his children with his ex-wife. The father, unhappy with the operation of the portion of the separation agreement that concerned the provision of information concerning the schooling of the children, sent a letter to the superintendent of schools demanding information about his children's activities and progress. The superintendent responded that the school would provide information to any person or organization the courts decided had a legal right to the information.[88]

After the exchange of more letters between the father and the superintendent, the district began mailing copies of the children's education records to him. However, the school refused to mail him duplicates of all school-related notices mailed to his ex-wife or carried home by his children.

After a series of appeals before the commissioner of education and the lower courts, the case finally was decided by the Second Circuit. For our purposes, the relevant issue presented was whether the father could sue for damages for the school district's violation of FERPA when it refused to provide him with copies of information sent to his ex-wife.

The Second Circuit held that the father was entitled to sue for these damages and that the school district had "tacitly conceded liability" for violating FERPA. The court then sent the case back to the lower federal court to determine the amount of damages to be awarded.[89]

Such judicial interpretation apparently affirms the right of a joint custodial parent to receive duplicate copies of all school information mailed to the other parent. This includes information ranging, as it did in this case, "from standardized test results and accident reports to notices about classroom parties and cafeteria menus."[90]

16. The Board of Education's Responsibilities

Policy

Beyond ensuring that information on students not be released to unauthorized individuals, FERPA gives boards of education additional responsibilities, including adoption of a policy on how the district will meet the act's requirements and implementing regulations. The policy must be in writing and a copy made available on request to a parent or eligible student.[1]

Such a policy must include

- Information on how the school district informs parents and students of their rights. This is consistent with the annual notification requirement (see "Requirements for Notification," p. 86).[2]
- Information on how a parent or eligible student may inspect and review education records[3]
- A statement that personally identifiable data will not be released from an education record without the prior written consent of the parent or eligible student, except under certain circumstances (see "Release of Records without Consent," p. 74)[4]
- A statement as to whether the district's policy permits disclosure of personally identifiable information, as permitted under the regulations, and, if so, a specification of the criteria for determining which parties are school officials and what the school district considers to be a legitimate educational interest[5]
- A statement that a record of disclosures will be maintained and that a parent or eligible student may inspect and review that record[6]
- A specification of the types of personally identifiable information the school district has designated as directory information[7]
- A statement that the district permits a parent or eligible student to request a correction of the student's education records, obtain a hearing and to add a statement to the record[8]

Included in the requirement concerning information on how a parent or eligible student may inspect and review education records is a procedure the parent or eligible student must follow to inspect and review the records;

a description of the circumstances under which the school district believes it has legitimate cause to deny a request for a copy of those records, "with an understanding that a district may not deny access to education records"; a list of the types and locations of education records maintained by the district and the titles and addresses of the officials responsible for the records; and a "statement of fees (if any)" for copying. For more details on providing copies, see "Inspection and Review," page 80.[9]

There are some limitations on the right to inspect and review records. For instance, if the education records of a student contain information on more than one student, the parent or eligible student may inspect, review or be informed of only the specific information about that student.[10]

Requirements for Notification

Each school district must also annually notify parents of students currently in attendance and eligible students currently in attendance of their rights under FERPA and its regulations. The notice must include a statement that the parent or eligible student has a right to inspect and review the student's education records; request that records be amended to ensure that they are not inaccurate, misleading or otherwise in violation of the student's privacy or other rights; consent to disclosures of personally identifiable information contained in the records, except where the district may disclose without consent; file with U. S. Department of Education a complaint alleging failure of the district to comply with the act and regulations; and obtain a copy of the policy. The notice must also indicate where copies of the policy are located. A school district may provide the notice by any means that would be likely to inform the parents and eligible students of their rights.[11]

A district also must effectively notify parents of students who have a primary or home language other than English.[12]

Record Keeping

FERPA regulations require school districts to maintain a record of each request for access to the education records of each student and each disclosure of personally identifiable information from them. The district is required to keep this record with the student's education record for as long as the records are maintained.[13]

The record of each request or disclosure must include identification of the parties who have requested or received the personally identifiable information and "the legitimate interests the parties had in requesting or obtaining the information."[14]

If the district discloses personally identifiable information from an education record with the understanding that the party receiving the information may make further disclosures of the information, the record of the disclosure must include the names of the additional parties to whom the receiving party may disclose the information on behalf of the school district and the legitimate interests each of the additional parties has in requesting or obtaining the information.[15]

The regulations provide that the parent or eligible student and the school official or his or her assistants responsible for custody of the records may inspect the record of the request or disclosure relating to each student. No record need be made if the request was from or the disclosure made to the parent or eligible student, an authorized school official, a party with a written consent from the parent or eligible student or a party seeking directory information.[16]

Destruction of Records

The school district is not permitted to destroy any education records while there is an outstanding request to inspect and review them. The Department of Education has stated, however, that a school district is not required to honor a "standing request" for access to copies, although it may do so if it wishes. "If parents wish to obtain information from their child's records on a regular basis, they should submit such requests periodically."[17]

In New York State the destruction of records of a local government by a school district is subject to regulations of the commissioner of education. These regulations are explained in chapter 13.

17. Enforcement Procedures

FERPA requires the U. S. secretary of education to establish or designate an office and review board within the Department of Education to investigate, process, review and adjudicate violations of the act and complaints alleging violations that may be filed. The secretary has designated the Family Policy and Regulations Office of the Department of Education with the responsibility for investigating, processing and reviewing complaints and providing technical assistance to ensure compliance, with a right of review to the Education Appeal Board (see below).[1]

A school district is responsible for notifying the Family Policy and Regulations Office if the district determines it cannot comply with the act or its regulations because of a conflict with state or local law. The district must notify the office within 45 days and provide the text and the citation for the conflicting law.[2]

The complaint procedure is relatively simple. When the complaint is sent to the office, it must contain "specific allegations of fact giving reasonable cause to believe that a violation of the Act or regulations" has occurred. The office investigates each timely complaint to determine whether there has been a violation.[3]

When the office receives a complaint, it notifies the school district involved, in writing, that the complaint has been received. The notice will include the substance of the alleged violation and will inform the district that the office will investigate the complaint and that the district may submit a written response to the complaint.[4]

The office then reviews the complaint and response and may, at its discretion, permit the parties to submit further oral or written arguments or information.[5]

Following the investigation, the office provides the complainant and the school district with a written notice of its findings and its basis for them. If the office finds the district has not complied with the act or regulations, the notice will include a statement of the specific steps the district must take to comply and provide a "reasonable period of time, given all of the circumstances of the case" during which the district may voluntarily comply.[6]

If, after a subsequent investigation, the secretary finds the district has complied voluntarily during the time established as "reasonable," he or she will provide the complainant and the district with a written notice of the decision and the basis for the decision.[7]

What if the district fails to comply?

In such situations, the secretary of education may choose from among a number of options, sometimes depending upon the program under which the notice is issued. Available options include issuing a notice of intent to terminate funds; issuing a notice to withhold funds; or issuing a notice to cease and desist.[8]

The Education Appeal Board has jurisdiction to "conduct withholding or termination hearings initiated by Department of Education officials in connection with any applicable program." In addition, a recipient of funds who receives a written notice from an authorized department official of an intent to withhold or terminate funds is entitled to a review by an Education Appeal Board Panel.[9]

Although it has been held by several courts that, given FERPA's extensive enforcement mechanism,[10] an individual cannot sue on his or her own behalf to have FERPA's provisions enforced (no such private cause of action exists), school districts should be advised that in *Fay* (see chap. 15, p. 83), a federal Court of Appeals acknowledged an individual's right to file a federal civil rights lawsuit to have these rights enforced.[11] In so holding, the court stated the lower court had "correctly determined that FERPA creates an interest that may be vindicated in a [civil rights] action because Congress did not create so comprehensive a system of enforcing the statute as to demonstrate an intention to preclude a remedy under [the civil rights statute]. Although FERPA recognizes extensive enforcement procedures created by regulation, these regulations do not demonstrate a Congressional intent to preclude suits . . . to remedy violations of FERPA."[12]

In most instances, the damages suffered by an individual because of a school district's violation of FERPA would probably be minimal, but a district's liability for attorneys' fees and punitive damages could be substantial.

18. Other Relevant Federal and State Laws and Regulations

Other federal and state statutes and regulations contain information related to access to student records. Because generally these provisions are not as universally applicable or as commonly invoked as FERPA, we will not delve into them in as much detail.

Federal Statutes and Regulations

One federal statute that has important provisions concerning student records is the Education of All Handicapped Children Act of 1975.[1] Parents or guardians of such students are guaranteed certain procedural safeguards concerning the provision of a free appropriate public education. Among the procedures is an "opportunity for the parents or guardian of a child with a disability to examine all relevant records with respect to the identification, evaluation, and educational placement of the child, and the provision of a free appropriate public education to such child."[2]

While the act provides that the secretary of education shall collect data concerning programs and projects carried out under the statute, including information relating to "handicapped infants, toddlers, children and youth," the secretary also is empowered to "take appropriate action, in accordance with the provisions of [FERPA], to assure the protection of the confidentiality of any personally identifiable data, information, and records collected or maintained by the Secretary and by State and local educational agencies" pursuant to the act.[3]

The secretary's implementing regulations contain a comprehensive section on the confidentiality of information. Included are the requirements that the state educational agency (in New York State, the State Education Department) give notice informing parents of information such as a description of the children on whom personally identifiable data is maintained, the kinds of information sought, the methods the state plans to use in gathering the information (including sources from whom information is gathered) and the use to be made of the information. The agency also must provide parents with a summary of the policies and procedures school districts must follow concerning the storage, disclosure to third parties, retention and destruction of personally identifiable information.[4]

The agency must give parents "a description of all of the rights of parents and children regarding this information, including the rights under [FERPA] and [its implementing regulations]."[5]

The regulations specifically require school districts to allow parents to inspect "any education records relating to their children which are collected, maintained, or used" by the district under the regulations. The district must comply with the request "without unnecessary delay and before any meeting regarding an individualized education program or hearing relating to the identification, evaluation, or placement of the child, and in no case more than 45 days after the request has been made."[6]

It should be noted the requirement stipulating a 45-day period between the request and its fulfillment matches that mandated under FERPA. In addition, rights of inspection and review parallel those identified in FERPA: the right to a response from the district to reasonable requests for explanations and interpretations of the records; the right to request copies of the records if failure to provide those copies would effectively prevent the parent from exercising the right to inspect and review and the right to have a representative of the parent inspect and review the record.[7]

The district may presume the parent has the authority to inspect and review the records concerning his or her child unless it has been advised that he or she "does not have the authority under applicable state law governing such matters as guardianship, separation, and divorce." This is also consistent with FERPA.[8]

Each district is also required to keep a record of parties obtaining access to education records and provide requesting parents with a list of the types and locations of education records collected, maintained, or used by the district. The act also contains provisions, similar to those enumerated in the FERPA regulations, concerning a parent's right to amend records, the opportunity for a hearing to challenge information in education records "to insure that it is not inaccurate, misleading or otherwise in violation of the privacy or other rights of the child," hearing procedures and how the result of a hearing is to be handled.[9]

A school district must have parental consent before it provides personally identifiable information to anyone other than officials of the district collecting or using the information pursuant to the regulations or when the information is to be used for any purpose other than meeting one of the regulation's requirements. In addition, school districts may not release information from education records to other districts without parental consent unless authorized under the FERPA regulations.[10]

The state educational agency is required to include policies and procedures in its annual program plan to be used if a parent should refuse to provide consent under the regulations.[11]

Each school district is required to protect the confidentiality of personally identifiable information and must appoint an official with the responsibility of ensuring the confidentiality of all personally identifiable information. Training for anyone collecting or using personally identifiable information regarding a state's policies and procedures in this area and under the FERPA regulations is also mandated. A current list of those employees with access to this information must be available for public inspection.[12]

The regulations also require districts to inform a child's parents when personally identifiable information is no longer needed to provide educational services for him or her. Such information must be destroyed at the request of the parents, but a permanent record of a student's name, address, telephone number, grades, attendance record, classes attended, grade level completed and year completed may be permanently maintained.[13]

The state educational agency also is required to include policies and procedures in its annual program plan concerning the extent to which children are afforded rights of privacy similar to those afforded parents, "taking into consideration the age of child and type or severity of disability." This provision differs somewhat from the FERPA regulations, where the rights of parents are transferred to students at the age of 18.[14]

State Regulations

The regulations of the commissioner of education concerning the education of pupils and preschool children with handicapping conditions in private schools and state-operated or state-supported schools contain a provision stating the confidentiality of student records will be maintained and that parental access to these records will be permitted "in a manner comparable to that required of school districts" pursuant to FERPA. Thus, for these students, confidentiality of such records must be maintained, even though the students are not in the public schools.[15]

Appendix

SAMPLE POLICIES

These policies were developed by the Office of Policy, Employee Relations and Risk Management Services of the New York State School Boards Association and are contained in *Law and Management Policies for Schools* (*LAMPS*), a publication of New York School Boards Association. For more information, call (518) 465-3474 or 1 800 342-3360.

These sample policies are related to the Open Meetings Law

LAMPS Sample Policy 2330

EXECUTIVE SESSIONS

The Board of Education reserves the right, within the constraints of State Law, to meet in executive session. Such sessions can be requested by any member of the Board or the Superintendent of Schools.

Upon a majority vote of its members, the Board may convene an executive session to discuss the subjects enumerated below. Matters which may be considered in executive session are:

1. matters which will imperil the public safety if disclosed;
2. any matter which may disclose the identity of a law enforcement agent or informer;
3. information relating to current or future investigation or prosecution of a criminal offense which would imperil effective law enforcement if disclosed;
4. discussions regarding proposed, pending or current litigation;
5. collective negotiations pursuant to Article 14 of the Civil Service Law (the Taylor Law);
6. medical, financial, credit or employment history of a particular person or corporation, or matters leading to the appointment, employment, promotion, demotion, discipline, suspension, dismissal or removal of a particular person or corporation;
7. the preparation, grading or administration of examinations; and
8. the proposed acquisition, sale, or lease of real property or the proposed acquisition of securities, or sale or exchange of securities, but only when publicity would substantially affect the value thereof.

Matters which may *only* be considered in executive session are:

9. discussions concerning probable cause to bring disciplinary charges against a tenured teacher; and
10. discussions concerning findings and/or placement of students by the Committee on Special Education.

Formal action or vote on matters enumerated in paragraphs 9 and 10 above may only be taken by the Board during an executive session. No formal action or vote may be taken on any other matter. The Board shall reconvene in open session to take final action on other matters discussed, and to adjourn the meeting.

Minutes of executive sessions will reflect all actions and votes taken by the Board in executive session without personally identifying employees or students affected thereby. The name of the person who called for the executive session will also appear in the minutes of the public meeting. The Board may permit staff and other persons whose presence is deemed necessary or appropriate to attend an executive session or any part thereof.

Ref: Education Law §§1708 (3); 3020-a (2)
     Public Officers Law §§100 et seq.
     Formal Opinion of Counsel to the State Education Department No. 239

LAMPS **Sample Policy 2360**

MINUTES

The Board of Education believes that open and accurate communication regarding its internal operations enhances the district's public relations program and provides a record of the district's progress towards its annual goals.

Therefore, the Board will maintain a complete and accurate set of minutes of each meeting. Such minutes shall constitute the official record of proceedings of the Board and shall be open to public inspection within one week of executive sessions and within two weeks of all other meetings.

All motions, proposals, resolutions, and any other matters formally voted upon by the Board shall be recorded in Board minutes. In recording such votes, the names of the Board members shall be called in alphabetical order, and the record shall indicate the final vote of each Board member.

If a Board member is not present at the opening of a meeting, the subsequent arrival time of such member shall be indicated in the minutes.

A draft of the minutes of each meeting is to be forwarded to each member of the Board not later than the time the agenda for the next meeting is disseminated.

Minutes are public documents and thus shall be open to inspection by the public.

Ref: Open Meetings Law, Public Officers Law §§100 et seq.
      Freedom of Information Law, Public Officers Law §§84 et seq.
      Education Law §2121

This sample policy is related to the Freedom of Information Law

LAMPS Sample Policy 1120

SCHOOL DISTRICT RECORDS

It is the policy of the Board of Education to inform members of the public about the administration and operation of the public schools in accordance with the Freedom of Information Law of the State of New York.

The Superintendent of Schools shall develop and submit to the Board for approval, regulations ensuring compliance with the Freedom of Information Law and governing the procedures to be followed to obtain access to district records. The Superintendent shall designate, with Board approval, Records Access and Records Management Officers, pursuant to law.

Retention and Destruction of Records:

The Board of Education hereby adopts as policy the Records Retention and Disposition Schedules as promulgated by the Commissioner of Education, setting forth the minimum length of time school district records must be retained.

Ref: Public Officers Law §84 et seq.
     Education Law §2116
     Arts and Cultural Affairs Law §57.11
     Local Government Records Law, Article 57-A
     8 NYCRR Part 185

LAMPS Sample Regulation 1120-R

SCHOOL DISTRICT RECORDS REGULATION

The following comprises the rules and regulations relating to the inspection and copying of school district records:

I. *Designation of Officers:*
   1. The Records Access Officer shall be the School Business Manager.
   2. The Records Access Officer is designated to receive requests for records of the Board of Education and make such records available for inspection or copying when such requests are granted.
   3. The Records Access Officer shall compile and maintain a detailed current list by subject matter, of all records in the possession of the Board, whether or not available to the public.
   4. The Superintendent, with the Board's approval, shall designate a Records Management Officer for the district.
   5. The Records Management Officer will develop and oversee a program for the orderly and efficient management of district records.

II. *Definition of Records:*
   1. A record is defined as any information kept, held, filed, produced or reproduced by, with or for the Board in any physical form whatsoever, including but not limited to reports, statements, examinations, memoranda, opinions, folders, files, books, manuals, pamphlets, forms, papers, designs, drawings, maps, photos, letters, microfilms, computer tapes or disks, rules, regulations or codes.
   2. The Records Access Officer will have the responsibility for compiling and maintaining the following records:
      a. a record of the final vote of each member of the Board on any proceeding or matter on which the member votes;
      b. a record setting forth the name, school or office address, title and salary of every officer or employee of the Board. Such records shall be made available for inspection under the supervision of the Records Access Officer; and
      c. a detailed current list by subject matter of all records in possession of the Board, whether or not available for public inspection and copying.
   3. No record for which there is a pending request for access may be destroyed. However, nothing in these regulations shall require the Board to prepare any record not possessed or maintained by it except the records specified in II(2), above.

III. *Access to Records*
   1. Time and place records may be inspected: Records may be requested from, and inspected or copied at, the Office of the Records Access Officer, or at a location specified by the Records Access Officer, during regular business hours on any business day on which the Board of Education offices are open.
   2. Fees: The fee for documents up to 8½ x 14 inches is 25 cents per page. For documents larger than 8½ x 14 inches, tape or cassette records, or computer printouts, the cost will be based on the cost of reproduction or program utilized. Fees are subject to periodic review and change. However, no fee shall be charged for search for or inspection of records, certification of documents, or copies of documents which have been printed or reproduced for distribution to the public. The number of such copies given to any one organization or individual may be limited, in the discretion of the Records Access Officer.
   3. Procedures: Requests to inspect or secure copies of records shall be submitted in writing, either in person or by mail, to the Records Access Officer.
   4. All requests for information shall be responded to within five business days of receipt of the request. If the request cannot be fulfilled within five business days, the Records Access Officer shall acknowledge receipt of the request and advise the approximate date when the request will be granted or denied.
   5. Denial of Access: When a request for access to a public record is denied, the Records Access Officer shall indicate in writing the reasons for such denial, and the right to appeal.
   6. Appeal: An applicant denied access to a public record may file an appeal by delivering a copy of the request and a copy of the denial to the district clerk of the Board within 30 days after the denial from which such appeal is taken.
   7. The appeal will be submitted to the Board for decision. The applicant and the Committee on Open Government will be informed of the Board's determination in writing within ten business days of receipt of an appeal. The district clerk shall transmit to the New York State Committee on Open Government photocopies of all appeals and determinations.

IV. *Records Exempted from Public Access:*
   The provisions of this regulation relating to information available for public inspection and copying shall not apply to records that:
   1. are specifically exempted from disclosure by state and/or federal statute;
   2. if disclosed would constitute an unwarranted invasion of personal

privacy;

3. if disclosed would impair present or imminent contract awards or collective bargaining negotiations;

4. are confidentially disclosed to the Board and compiled and maintained for the regulation of commercial enterprise, including trade secrets, or for the grant or review of a license;

5. are compiled for law enforcement purposes and which, if disclosed, would:

   a. interfere with law enforcement investigations or judicial proceedings;

   b. deprive a person of a right to a fair trial or impartial adjudication;

   c. identify a confidential source or disclose confidential techniques or procedures, except routine techniques or procedures; or

   d. reveal criminal investigative techniques or procedures, except routine techniques and procedures;

6. records which if disclosed would endanger the life or safety of any person;

7. records which are interagency or intra-agency communications, except to the extent that such materials consist of:

   a. statistical or factual tabulations or data;

   b. instructions to staff which affect the public;

   c. final Board policy determinations; or

   d. external audits, including but not limited to audits performed by the comptroller and the federal government;

8. records which are examination questions or answers that are requested prior to the final administration of such questions;

9. records which are computer access codes.

V. *Prevention of Unwarranted Invasion of Privacy*

To prevent an unwarranted invasion of personal privacy, the Records Access Officer may delete identifying details when records are made available. An unwarranted invasion of personal privacy includes but shall not be limited to:

1. disclosure of confidential personal matters reported to the Board which are not relevant or essential to the ordinary work of the Board;

2. disclosure of employment, medical or credit histories or personal references of applicants for employment, unless the applicant has provided a written release permitting such disclosures;

3. sale or release of lists of names and addresses in the possession of the Board if such lists would be used for private, commercial or fund-raising purposes;

4. disclosure of information of a personal nature when disclosure would result in economic or personal hardship to the subject party and such records are not relevant or essential to the ordinary work of the Board; or
5. disclosure of items involving the medical or personal records of a client or patient in a hospital or medical facility.

Unless otherwise deniable, disclosure shall not be construed to constitute an unwarranted invasion of privacy when identifying details are deleted, when the person to whom records pertain consents in writing to disclosure, or when upon representing reasonable proof of identify, a person seeks access to records pertaining to him or her.

LAMPS **Sample Exhibit 1120-E**

SCHOOL DISTRICT RECORDS EXHIBIT

<u>Application for Public Access to Records</u>

To: Records Access Officer _____
     Board of Education
     School District
     New York

I hereby apply to inspect only or inspect and request reproduction of

the following record @ 25 cents per page: _____

Signature _____ Date _____

I hereby acknowledge receipt of the reproduction of records.

Signature _____ Date _____

Mailing Address _____

FOR OFFICE USE ONLY

Approved [   ]

Denied (for the reason(s) checked below)

[   ] Confidential disclosure
[   ] Part of investigatory files
[   ] Unwarranted invasion of personal privacy
[   ] Record of which this agency is legal custodian cannot be found
[   ] Record is not maintained by this agency
[   ] Exempted by statute other than the Freedom of Information Act
[   ] Other (specify) _____

Signature/Title _____ Date _____

LAMPS **Sample Exhibit 1120-E**

SCHOOL DISTRICT RECORDS EXHIBIT

(continued)

NOTICE: You Have A Right To Appeal A Denial Of This Application To
        The Head of This Agency:
                    Superintendent of Schools
                    School District

        Who Must Fully Explain His/Her Reasons For Such Denial In
        Writing Within Ten Days of Receipt Of An Appeal.

I hereby appeal _____

Signature   Date

This sample policy is related to the Family Educational Rights and Privacy Act

LAMPS **Sample Policy 5500**

STUDENT RECORDS

The Board of Education recognizes the legal requirement to maintain the confidentiality of student records. The procedures for the confidentiality of student records shall be consistent with federal statutes, including the Family Educational Rights and Privacy Act of 1974 (FERPA) and its implementing regulations, and the Commissioner's Regulations.

The Superintendent of Schools shall be responsible for ensuring that all requirements under federal statutes and Commissioner's Regulations shall be carried out by the district.

Annual Notification

At the beginning of each school year, the district shall publish in a local newspaper a notice to parent(s) or guardian(s) of students under 18 years of age and students 18 years of age or older ("eligible students") currently in attendance of their rights under FERPA and this policy. The district shall also send home a bulletin listing these rights, which will also be included with a packet of material provided parents or an eligible student when the student enrolls during the school year.

The notice must include a statement that the parent or eligible student has a right to:

1. inspect and review the student's education records;
2. a specification of the intent of the school district to limit the disclosure of personally identifiable information contained in a student's education records except:
   a. by prior written consent of the student's parent(s) or guardian(s) or the eligible student;
   b. as directory information; or
   c. under certain limited circumstances, as permitted by FERPA.
3. request that records be amended to ensure that they are not inaccurate, misleading, or otherwise in violation of the student's privacy or other rights;
4. file a complaint with the U.S. Department of Education alleging failure of the district to comply with FERPA and its regulations; and
5. obtain copies of this policy and the locations where copies may be obtained.

The policy applicable to the release of student directory information applies equally to military recruiters, the media, colleges and universities, and prospective employers.

The district shall arrange to provide translations of this notice to non-English speaking parents in their native language.

<u>Cross-ref</u>: 1120, School District Records

<u>Ref</u>: Family Educational Rights and Privacy Act (FERPA) of 1974
20 USC 1232-g; 34 CFR Part 99
Education Law §§2(13); 225; 301

LAMPS **Sample Regulation 5500-R**

STUDENT RECORDS REGULATION

It is recognized that the confidentiality of pupil records must be maintained. The following necessary procedures have been adopted to guarantee the protection of pupil records.

Section 1. Pursuant to the "Family Educational Rights and Privacy Act of 1974" it shall be the policy of this school district with respect to parents of a student under 18 years of age and with respect to students 18 years of age or older (an "eligible student") to permit such persons to inspect and review any and all official records, files and data directly related to that student, including all materials that are incorporated into each student's cumulative record folder, and intended for school use or to be available to parties outside the school or school system, and specifically including, but not necessarily limited to, identifying data, academic work completed, level of achievement (grades, standardized achievement test scores), attendance data, scores on standardized intelligence, aptitude, and psychological tests, interest inventory results, health data, family background information, teacher or counselor ratings and observations, and verified reports of serious or recurrent behavior patterns.

Section 2. Parents of a student under 18 years of age or an eligible student shall have an opportunity for a hearing to challenge the content of that student's school records, to insure that the records are not inaccurate, misleading, or otherwise in violation of the privacy or other rights of students, and to provide an opportunity for the correction or deletion of any such inaccurate, misleading, or otherwise inappropriate data contained therein.

Section 3. In order to implement the rights provided for in Sections 1 and 2 hereof, the following procedures are adopted:

(a) A parent of a student under 18 years of age or an eligible student shall make a request for access to that student's school records, in writing, to the Superintendent of Schools. Upon receipt of such request, arrangements shall be made to provide access to such records within thirty (30) days after the request has been received.

(b) A parent of a student under 18 years of age or an eligible student, who wishes to challenge the contents of that student's school records, shall submit a request, in writing, identifying the record or records which they believe to be inaccurate, misleading or otherwise in violation of the privacy or other rights of the student together with a statement with the reasons for their challenge to the record to the Superintendent.

(c) Upon receipt of a written challenge, the Superintendent shall provide a written response indicating either that he/she finds the challenged record inaccurate, misleading or otherwise in violation and it will be corrected or deleted, or that he/she finds no basis for correcting or deleting the record in question, but that the parent or eligible student will be given an opportunity for a hearing. Such written response by the Superintendent shall be provided the parent or eligible student within fourteen (14) days after receipt of the written challenge. Said response shall also outline the procedures to be followed with respect to a hearing, if desired by the parent or eligible student.

(d) Within fourteen (14) days of receipt of the response from the Superintendent a parent or eligible student may request, in writing, that a hearing be held to review the determination of the Superintendent.

Section 4. Student records, and any material contained herein which is personally identifiable, are confidential and may not be released or made available to persons other than parents or students without the written consent of parents of students 18 years of age or younger. Such records and material may be made available without the written consent of parents or eligible students in the following cases:

1. to other school officials, including teachers within the district who have legitimate educational interests;
2. to officials of another school in which the student intends to enroll, if the parents or student are notified of the transfer of records, are given a copy if they desire one, and have an opportunity for a hearing to challenge the content of the records;
3. to authorized representatives of certain designated federal and state agencies, including state educational authorities, for the purpose of the audit and in connection with the enforcement of federal legal requirements;
4. in connection with a student's application for or receipt of financial aid; and
5. pursuant to court order or subpoena, after notification to the parent or eligible student.

Section 5. Whenever a student record or any material contained therein is to be made available to third persons, other than those covered by the exceptions indicated in Section 4 hereof, the parent of a student under 18 years of age or an eligible student must file a written consent to such action and any third party to whom such records have been made available must sign a written statement that he will not further release such records without the consent of the parent or eligible student.

Section 6. All persons requesting access to such records except for those persons provided for in subdivision 1 of Section 4 hereof, state agencies provided for in subdivision 3 of Section 4 hereof and those persons provided for in subdivision 5 of Section 4 hereof shall be required to sign a written form which indicates a legitimate educational or other interest that such person has in inspecting the records. Such form shall be kept with the student's file. See Exhibit 5500-E.2.

Section 7. Whenever the district is requested to forward a student's school records, including health records, to a neighboring public school district within this BOCES, the following procedures shall be followed:
1. A student's school records, including health records, shall be forwarded to the neighboring public school district from which such a request is made upon the receipt of a request by the appropriate administrator of the requesting district.
2. The prior written consent of the student's parents or eligible student shall not be necessary. However, upon the forwarding of the student's records, the parent(s) of the student or eligible student shall be notified in writing that the records have been transferred.

Such notice shall be by certified letter, return receipt requested and such letter shall be forwarded to the parents or eligible student not later than the close of business of the day upon which the student's records are forwarded to the neighboring district.

Section 8. All instructional material, including teachers' manuals, which are used in connection with a research or experimental program must be available for inspection by the parents or guardians of the children engaged in such program. "Research or experimentation program or project" is defined as a program or project "designed to explore or develop new or unproven teaching methods or techniques."

Section 9. A letter shall be sent to parents of students under 18 years of age and to eligible students informing them of their rights pursuant to the "Family Educational Rights and Privacy Act of 1974." See Exhibit 5500-E.1.

Dear Parent or Student:

   This is to advise you of your rights with respect to the school records relating to (your son) (your daughter) (you) pursuant to the Federal "Family Educational Rights and Privacy Act of 1974."

   Parents of a student under 18, or a student 18 or older, have a right to inspect and review any and all official records, files, and data directly related to their children, including all material that is incorporated into each student's cumulative record folder, and intended for school use or to be available to parties outside the school or school system, and specifically including, but not necessarily limited to, identifying data, academic work completed, level of achievement (grades, standardized achievement test scores), attendance data, scores on standardized intelligence, aptitude, and psychological tests, interest inventory results, health data, family background information, teacher or counselor ratings and observations, and verified reports of serious or recurrent behavior patterns.

   A parent of a student under 18 years of age or a student 18 years of age or older shall make a request for access to that student's school records, in writing, to the Superintendent of Schools. Upon receipt of such request, arrangements shall be made to provide access to such records within a reasonable period of time, but in any case, not more than forty-five (45) days after the request has been received.

   Such parents and students are also entitled to an opportunity for a hearing to challenge the content of such records, to insure that they are not inaccurate, misleading, or otherwise in violation of the privacy or other rights of students, and to provide an opportunity for the correction or deletion of any such inaccurate misleading, or otherwise inappropriate data contained therein. Any questions concerning the procedure to be followed in requesting such a hearing should be directed to the Superintendent.

   Student records, and any material contained therein which is personally identifiable, are confidential and may not be released or made available to persons other than parents or students without the written consent of such parents or student. There are a number of exceptions to this rule, such as other school employees and officials, and certain State and Federal officials, who have a legitimate educational need for access to such records in the course of their employment.

                              Sincerely yours,
                              SUPERINTENDENT OF SCHOOLS

LAMPS **Sample Exhibit 5500-E.2**

NOTIFICATION OF RELEASE OF STUDENT RECORDS PURSUANT TO COURT ORDER OR SUBPOENA

TO: _____

    Parent-Student

_____

_____

_____

    Address

    The purpose of this notice is to notify you that on _____ (date),

the _____ (school district) released the follow-

ing documents: _____

_____

_____

from your child's (your own) student records to _____

_____

pursuant to a court order or subpoena, a copy of which is attached hereto.

Signature _____ Date _____

LAMPS Sample Exhibit 5500-E.3

APPLICATION TO REVIEW STUDENT RECORDS BY PARTIES ENTITLED THERETO WITHOUT CONSENT OF PARENT OR STUDENT

I, _____

have hereby requested access to _____

_____ records for the following reasons:

_____

_____

Said records will not be made available to any other person or persons

without the specific consent of _____

(Parent-Student).

Signature _____ Date _____

LAMPS Sample Exhibit 5500-E.4

APPLICATION TO REVIEW STUDENT'S RECORDS AND CONSENT THERETO BY PARENT OR STUDENT

<u>APPLICATION</u>

I, _____

have hereby requested access to _____

_____ records for the following reasons:

_____

_____

Said records will not be made available to any other person or persons

without the specific consent of _____

(Parent-Student).

<u>CONSENT</u>

I hereby consent that _____

have access (to my child's) (to my) records with the understanding that such

LAMPS Sample Exhibit 5500-E.4

APPLICATION TO REVIEW STUDENT'S RECORDS
AND CONSENT THERETO BY PARENT OR STUDENT
(continued)

records will not be released by him/her to other persons without my

further consent.

Signature_____Date_____

Notes

Part 1. The Open Meetings Law

Chapter 1. Introduction

1. Laws of 1976, chap. 511, effective January 1, 1977.
2. *Holden v. Board of Trustees of Cornell University*, 440 NYS 2d 58, *aff'd* 80 AD2d 378 (3d Dept., 1978); Public Officers Law §100.
3. *Goodson-Todman Enterprises Ltd. v. City of Kingston Common Council*, 153 AD2d 103, 105 (3d Dept., 1990), quoting *Matter of Orange County Publications, Division of Ottoway Newspapers, Inc., v. Council of the City of Newburgh*, 60 AD2d 409, 414, *aff'd* 45 NY2d 947 (1978).
4. *Orange County Publications v. Newburgh*, 45 NY2d 947, 949 (1978).
5. Public Officers Law §89 (1)(a).
6. *Ibid.*, §§89, 93.
7. *Sciolino v. Ryan*, 103 Misc. 2d 1021, *aff'd* 81 AD2d 475 (4th Dept. 1981); *County of Saratoga v. Newman*, 124 Misc. 2d 626 (Sup. Ct., Saratoga Co. 1984).
8. *Matter of John P. v. Whalen*, 54 NY2d 89, 95-96 (1981).
9. Public Officers Law §103(a).
10. *Ibid.*, §103(b).
11. *Ibid.*, Article 4-A; 42 *United States Code* (hereafter cited as USC) §4151 *et seq.*
12. Public Buildings Law §52.
13. 9 *New York Code of Rules and Regulations* (hereafter cited as NYCRR) part 1100 *et seq.*
14. Public Officers Law §74-a.
15. Open Meetings Law §102.
16. *Orange County Publications v. Newburgh*, 60 AD2d 409, *aff'd* 45 NY2d 947 (1978).
17. Laws of 1979, chap. 704, effective October 1, 1979.
18. Public Officers Law §102.
19. General Construction Law §66; see Education Law §1950; and Open Meetings Law-Advisory Opinion of the Committee on Open Government (hereafter cited as OML-AO)-740 (March 22, 1982).
20. Public Officers Law §102.

Chapter 2. Covered Bodies

1. General Construction Law §66.
2. Public Officers Law §102(2).
3. See *ibid.*; and General Construction Law §66.
4. *Kamlet v. Board of Education, Plainedge Union Free School District*, 91 Misc. 2d 1105 (Sup. Ct., Nassau Co. 1977).
5. *Matter of Orange County Publications, Division of Ottoway Newspapers, Inc., v. Council of the City of Newburgh*, 60 AD2d 409, 416-17 (2d Dept. 1978).

6. *Daily Gazette Co., Inc., v. North Colonie Board of Education*, 67 AD2d 803 (3d Dept. 1978).

7. See, e.g., *Sciolino v. Ryan*, 103 Misc. 2d 1021, *aff'd* 81 AD2d 475 (4th Dept. 1981); and *Matter of Gannett Co. v. City of Rochester*, 83 AD2d 755 (4th Dept. 1981).

8. See, e.g., *Poughkeepsie Newspaper v. Mayor's Intergovernmental Task Force on New York City Water Supply Needs*, 145 AD2d 65 (2d Dept. 1989); *Goodson-Todman Enterprises Ltd. v. Town Board of Milan*, 151 AD2d 642 (2d Dept. 1989); and *NYPIRG v. Governor's Advisory Commission*, 135 AD2d 1149 (1st Dept. 1988).

9. General Construction Law §41.

10. Public Officers Law §102(2).

11. OML-AO- _____, (April 17, 1991).

Chapter 3. Covered Meetings

1. *Goodson-Todman Enterprises Ltd. v. City of Kingston Common Council*, 153 AD2d 103 (3d Dept. 1990).

2. *Matter of Orange County Publications, Division of Ottoway Newspapers, Inc., v. Council of the City of Newburgh*, 60 AD2d 409, *aff'd* 45 NY2d 947 (1978).

3. *Puka v. Greco*, 119 Misc. 2d 696, *aff'd* 104 AD2d 362 (2d Dept. 1984).

4. *Goodson-Todman v. Kingston*, 153 AD2d 103, 105 (3d Dept. 1990).

5. *Oneonta Star, Division of Ottoway Newspapers, Inc., v. Board of Trustees of Oneonta School District*, 66 AD2d 51 (3d Dept. 1979).

6. *Orange County Publications v. Newburgh*, 60 AD2d 409, 417, *aff'd* 45 NY2d 947 (1978).

7. *Matter of Britt v. County of Niagara*, 82 AD2d 65, 68 (4th Dept. 1981).

8. *Matter of Buffalo Evening News, Inc., v. Buffalo Municipal Housing Authority*, 134 Misc. 2d 155, 157 (Sup. Ct., Erie Co. 1986); and *Matter of Tri-Village Publishers v. St. Johnsville Board of Education*, 110 AD2d 932, 933 (3d Dept. 1985).

9. *Buffalo Evening News v. Buffalo Housing Authority*, 134 Misc. 2d 155, 158 (Sup. Ct., Erie Co. 1986).

10. *Goodson-Todman v. Kingston*, 153 AD2d 103, 105 (3d Dept. 1990).

11. *Orange County Publications v. Newburgh*, 60 AD2d 409, 415-19, *aff'd* 45 NY2d 947 (1978).

12. *Ibid.*, 60 Ad2d, 416.

13. *Matter of Binghamton Press Company, Inc., v. Board of Education of the City School District of the City of Binghamton*, 67 AD2d 797, 798 (3d Dept. 1979); *Koerner v. Board of Education, Deer Park Union Free School District*, 61 AD2d 796 (2d Dept. 1978).

14. See *Goodson-Todman v. Kingston*, 153 AD2d 103, 105 (3d Dept. 1990).

15. Public Officers Law §108(1)(2).

16. *Matter of Spink*, 25 Educ. Dept. Rep. 310 (1986).

17. Public Officers Law §108(3).

18. *Ibid.*; however, once the attorney has provided legal advice and a board continues its deliberations, the attorney-client relationship would cease, and the Open Meetings Law would again apply.

19. 20 USC §1232(g).

20. For a more complete discussion of FERPA, see part 3.

21. Public Officers Law §108(3).

22. 8 NYCRR §200.7(b)(2); 20 USC §1232(g).

23. For a further discussion of the exception, see "Mandatory Subjects for Executive Session," p. 32.

24. *Orange County Publications v. Newburgh*, 60 AD2d 409, 416 (1978).

25. *Kessel v. D'Amato*, 97 Misc. 2d 675 (Sup. Ct., Nassau Co. 1979).

26. *Sciolino v. Ryan*, 103 Misc. 2d 1021, *aff'd* 81 AD2d 475 (4th Dept. 1981).

Chapter 4. Notice of Meetings

1. Public Officers Law §104.

2. Education Law §§1606, 1708, 2504.

3. Public Officers Law §104(1).

4. *Ibid.*, §104(2).

5. *White v. Battaglia*, 79 AD2d 880 (4th Dept. 1980), *appeal denied* 53 NY2d 603 (1980).

6. *Britt v. County of Niagara*, 82 AD2d 65, 69-70 (4th Dept. 1979); *Village of Philmont v. X-Tyal International Corp.*, 67 AD2d 1039 (3d Dept. 1979).

7. *Monroe-Livingston Sanitary Landfill, Inc., v. Bickford*, 107 AD2d 1062, 1063 (4th Dept. 1985).

8. *Matter of Colasuonno*, 22 Educ. Dept. Rep. 215 (1982).

9. *Matter of Carlson*, 11 Educ. Dept. Rep. 284 (1972).

10. Education Law §1708.

11. *Ibid.*, §2504.

12. *Ibid.*, §1606.

13. Ibid., §2504.

14. Public Officers Law §104 (2); see also *Matter of White v. Battaglia*, 79 AD2d 880, *leave denied*, 53 NY2d 603.

Chapter 5. Procedures at Meetings

1. Henry M. Roberts III and William J. Evans, eds., *Robert's Rules of Order, Newly Revised* (Glenview, Ill.: Scott Foresman and Company, 1990).

2. *Matter of Miller and Cerniglia*, 17 Educ. Dept. Rep. 275 (1978).

3. *Matter of Kramer*, 72 Educ. Dept. Rep. 114 (1951).

4. Public Officers Law §100.

5. *Matter of Thomas*, 10 Educ. Dept. Rep. 108 (1971).

6. *Mitchell v. Board of Education of Garden City Union Free School District*, 113 AD2d 924 (2d Dept. 1985).

7. *Ibid.*, 113 AD2d 925 (2d Dept. 1985).

8. *Ibid.*

9. *People v. Ystueta*, 99 Misc. 2d 1105 (Sup. Ct., Suffolk Co. 1979).

10. *Matter of Davidson v. Common Council of the City of White Plains*, 40 Misc. 2d 1053

(Sup. Ct., Westchester Co. 1963); Op. St. Compt. 78-457 (June 5, 1978).

11. *Feldman v. Town of Bethel*, 106 AD2d 695, 697 (3d Dept. 1984).

12. OML-AO-790 (July 8, 1982).

13. OML-AO-1602 (August 27, 1984).

14. See, e.g., Education Law §§702, 3016(2); and General Municipal Law §802.

15. Public Officers Law §§87(3)(a), 106(1)(2).

16. General Construction Law §41.

17. See, e.g., *Downing v. Gaynor*, 47 Misc. 2d 535 (Sup. Ct., Nassau Co. 1965); *Rockland Woods, Inc., v. Suffern*, 40 AD2d 385 (2d Dept. 1973); *Walt Whitman Game Room, Inc., v. Zoning Board of Appeals*, 54 AD2d 764 (2d Dept. 1976); *Reiff v. New York City Conciliation and Appeals Board*, 128 Misc. 2d 851 (Sup. Ct., New York Co. 1985); and *Bank of New York v. Irving Bank Corp.*, 140 Misc. 2d 508 (Sup. Ct., New York Co. 1988).

18. *Poughkeepsie Newspaper v. Mayor's Intergovernmental Task Force on New York City Water Supply Needs*, 145 AD2d 65 (2d Dept. 1989); and *Goodson-Todman Enterprises Ltd. v. Town Board of Milan*, 151 AD2d 642 (2d Dept. 1989).

19. Public Officers Law §102(2).

20. General Construction Law §41.

21. *Matter of Miller and Cerniglia*, 17 Educ. Dept. Rep. 275 (1978).

22. Education Law §3016(2).

23. General Municipal Law §802(i).

24. Education Law §§701, 702.

25. OML-AO-1694 (December 22, 1989).

26. *Ibid.*, pp. 2-3.

27. In contrast, §708 of the Not-for-Profit Corporation Law expressly authorizes board meetings and voting by means of a conference telephone of similar communications equipment; however, no such authorization for school boards currently exists.

28. *Smithson v. Ilion Housing Authority*, 130 AD2d 965, 967 (4th Dept. 1988), *aff'd* 72 NY2d 1034 (1988).

29. Public Officers Law §106(1).

30. *Ibid.*, §106(2).

31. Education Law §2121.

32. Public Officers Law §§87(2), 106(3). The Freedom of Information Law is more fully discussed in part 2.

33. Public Officers Law §106(2).

34. *Ibid.*, §84 *et seq.*

35. *Ibid.*, §87(3); see also OML-AO- ____ (April 5, 1991).

36. See *Robert's Rules of Order*, §§34, 47.

37. Education Law §1501-a.

Chapter 6. Executive Sessions

1. Public Officers Law §102(3).

2. *Matter of Orange County Publications, Division of Ottoway Newspapers, Inc., v. Council*

of the City of Newburgh, 60 AD2d 409, 417, *aff'd* 45 NY2d 947 (1978).

3. Public Officers Law §105(1).

4. *Sanna v. Lindenhurst*, 107 Misc. 2d 267, *modified on other grounds* 85 AD2d 157 (2d Dept. 1982), *aff'd* 58 NY2d 626 (1982); *Goodson-Todman Enterprises Ltd. v. City of Kingston Common Council*, 153 AD2d, 103, 106 (1990).

5. *Weatherwax v. Town of Stony Point*, 97 AD2d 840, 841 (2d Dept. 1983); and *Daily Gazette Co., Inc., v. Town Board, Town of Cobleskill*, 111 Misc. 2d 303, 304-5 (Sup. Ct., Schoharie Co. 1981).

6. *Daily Gazette v. Cobleskill*, 111 Misc. 2d 303, 304-5 (Sup. Ct., Schoharie Co. 1981).

7. Public Officers Law §105.

8. *Ibid.*, §105(1)(f).

9. *Previdi v. Hirsch*, 138 Misc. 2d 436, 438 (Sup. Ct., Westchester Co. 1986); at least one court has held that "personnel layoffs" are primarily a budgetary matter and are therefore inappropriate for discussion in executive session under the Open Meetings Law; see *Orange County Publications, Division of Ottoway Newspapers, Inc., v. City of Middletown*, unreported (Sup. Ct., Orange Co. 1978); see also "Action Prohibited in Executive Session," p. 33.

10. See Public Officers Law §105(1)(f); and *Kloepfer v. Commissioner of Education, 82 AD2d 974 (3d Dept. 1981), aff'd* 56 NY2d 687 (1981).

11. Education Law §3020-a(2).

12. See Public Officers Law §105(1)(h); and *Oneonta Star, Division of Ottoway Newspapers, Inc., v. Board of Trustees of the Oneonta School District*, 66 AD2d 51, 54 (3d Dept. 1979).

13. *Botwin v. Board of Education*, 114 Misc. 2d 291, 294-95, 300-1 (Sup. Ct., Suffolk Co. 1982).

14. Public Officers Law §105(1)(d).

15. *Matter of Concerned Citizens to Review Jefferson Valley Mall v. Town Board of the Town of Yorktown*, 83 AD2d 612 (2d Dept. 1981); *Weatherwax v. Town of Stony Point*, 97 AD2d 840 (2d Dept. 1983).

16. *Weatherwax v. Stony Point*, 97 AD2d 840, 841 (2d Dept. 1983).

17. Public Officers Law §105(1)(e).

18. *Matter of County of Saratoga*, 17 PERB ¶3033 (1948), *aff'd* 17 PERB ¶7010 (Sup. Ct., Saratoga Co. 1984).

19. *Ibid.*, p. 3055, fn. 3.

20. See, e.g., *Matter of Town of Dresden*, 17 PERB ¶3096 (1984); and *Glen Cove City School District*, 6 PERB ¶3004 (1973).

21. See, e.g., *Matter of Kursch v. Board of Education, Union Free School District No. 1*, 7 AD2d 922 (2d Dept. 1959); *United Teachers of Northport v. Northport Union Free School District*, 50 AD2d 897 (2d Dept. 1975), and Formal Opinion of Counsel No. 239, 16 Educ. Dept. Rep. 457 (1976).

22. Formal Opinion of Counsel No. 239, 16 Educ. Dept. Rep. 457, 460-64 (1976); *Matter of Cappa*, 14 Educ. Dept. Rep. 80 (1974).

23. Education Law §3020-a(3)(c); 8 NYCRR §82.9.

24. *Matter of Kursch v. Board of Education*, 7 AD2d 922 (2d Dept. 1959); *United Teachers*

of Northport v. Northport Union Free School District, 50 AD2d 897 (2d Dept. 1975), and Formal Opinion of Counsel No. 239, 16 Educ. Dept. Rep. 457 (1976).

25. 8 NYCRR §84.3; *Gustin v. Joiner*, 95 Misc. 2d 277, *aff'd* 68 AD2d 880 (2d Dept. 1979).

26. *Orange County Publications v. Middletown*, unreported (Sup. Ct., Orange Co. 1978).

27. Public Officers Law §105(2).

28. Laws of 1979, chap. 704, effective October 1, 1979, amended the existing definition of the term *public body* by inserting "or committee or subcommittee or other similar body of such public body."

29. *Matter of Thomas*, 10 Educ. Dept. Rep. 108 (1971).

30. Public Officers Law §106(3).

31. *Ibid.*

Chapter 7. Enforcing the Open Meetings Law

1. See Public Officers Law §107(1); and *Village of Philmont v. X-Tyal International Corp.*, 67 AD2d 1039, 1040 (3d Dept. 1979).

2. Civil Practice Law and Rules (hereafter cited as CPLR) §7801.

3. Education Law §301.

4. See, e.g., *Matter of Dixon*, 20 Educ. Dept. Rep. 31, 35 (1980); *Matter of Concerned Parents Assn., Wheatley Heights*, 20 Educ. Dept. Rep. 185, 187 (1980); *Matter of Baker*, 22 Educ. Dept. Rep. 43, 44 (1982); and *Matter of Strober*, 30 Educ. Dept. Rep. 4, 6 (1990).

5. See, e.g., Public Officers Law §107; *Sanna v. Lindenhurst*, 107 Misc. 2d 267, *modified on other grounds* 85 AD2d 157, *aff'd* 58 NY2d 626 (1982); and *Puka v. Greco*, 119 Misc. 2d 696, 702, *aff'd* 104 AD2d (2d Dept. 1984).

6. *Matter of New York University v. Whalen*, 46 NY2d 734, 735 (1978).

7. See, e.g., Public Officers Law §107(1) and *Parents Action Committee v. Community School Board 31*, unreported (Sup. Ct., Richmond Co. 1984).

8. *Goodson-Todman Enterprises Ltd. v. City of Kingston Common Council*, 153 AD2d 103 (3d Dept. 1990); and *Matter of Binghamton Press Company, Inc., v. Board of Education of the City School District of the City of Binghamton*, 67 AD2d 797 (3d Dept. 1979).

9. Public Officers Law §107(1).

10. See, e.g., *Bowen v. State Commission on Correction*, 104 AD2d 283 (3d Dept.1985); and *Matter of Britt v. County of Niagara*, 82 AD2d 65, 69-70 (4th Dept. 1981).

11. *Puka v. Greco*, 104 AD2d 362, 363 (2d Dept. 1984); and *New York University v.Whalen*, 46 NY2d 734 (1978).

12. *White v. Battaglia*, 79 AD2d 880 (4th Dept. 1980).

13. *Previdi v. Hirsch*, 138 Misc. 2d 436, 440 (Sup. Ct., Westchester Co. 1988).

14. *Gilbert v. Board of Education of the Bath Central School District*, unreported (Sup. Ct., Steuben Co. 1986).

15. *Woll v. Erie County Legislature*, 83 AD2d 792, 793, *aff'd* 53 NY2d 1030 (1981).

16. *Dombroske v. Board of Education, West Genesee School District*, 118 Misc. 2d 800, 803-4

(1983).

17. Public Officers Law §107(2).

18. *Goodson-Todman Enterprises v. Kingston*, 153 AD2d 103 (3d Dept. 1990).

19. *Dombroske v. Board of Education*, 118 Misc. 2d 800 (1983).

20. *Matter of Orange County Publications, Division of Ottoway Newspapers, Inc., v. County of Orange*, 120 AD2d 596, 597 (2d Dept. 1986).

21. Public Officers Law §107(3).

22. *Previdi v. Hirsch*, 138 Misc. 2d 436, 440 (Sup. Ct., Westchester Co. 1988).

23. *Village of Philmont v. X-Tyal International Corp.*, 67 AD2d 1039, 1040 (3d Dept. 1979).

Part 2. The Freedom of Information Law

Chapter 8. Introduction

1. Public Officers Law §84 *et seq.*

2. Laws of 1977, chap. 933, effective Jan. 1, 1978.

3. *Matter of Fink v. Lefkowitz*, 47 NY2d 567, 571 (1979); *Matter of Farbman & Sons v. New York City Hospitals Corp.*, 62 NY2d 75, 79 (1984).

4. Public Officers Law §86(3).

5. *Russo v. Nassau Community College*, 554 NYS 2d 774 (1990).

6. Public Officers Law §86(4).

7. *Russo v. Nassau Community College*, 554 NYS 2d 774 (1990).

8. *Matter of Warder v. Board of Regents of University of State of New York*, 97 Misc.2d 86 (1978).

9. 21 NYCRR §1401.

10. Public Officers Law §87(1)(b).

11. 21 NYCRR §1401; 8 NYCRR §185.

12. *Matter of Wattenmaker v. New York State Employees' Retirement System*, 95 AD2d 910 (3d Dept. 1983).

13. Public Officers Law §89(3).

14. Local Government Records Law Article 57-A.

15. Public Officers Law §87(1)(b)(iii); and 21 NYCRR §1401.8(c), (c)(2).

16. 21 NYCRR §1401.9.

17. Public Officers Law §87(3)(a)(b).

Chapter 9. Accessible Records

1. Public Officers Law §87(2).

2. *Matter of Duncan v. Savino*, 90 Misc. 2d 282, 284 (1977).

3. *Capital Newspapers v. Burns*, 67 NY2d 562, 566-67 (1986).

4. Public Officers Law §89(3).

5. *Matter of Gannett Co., Inc., v. County of Monroe*, 59 AD2d 309, 313 (4th Dept. 1977).

6. *Matter of Kryston v. East Ramapo* CSD, 77 AD2d 896, 897 (2d Dept. 1980).

Chapter 10. Exempt Records

1. Public Officers Law §87(2).
2. *Capital Newspapers v. Burns,* 67 NY2d 562, 567 (1986); and *Matter of John P. v. Whalen,* 54 NY2d 89,94 (1981).
3. *Capital Newspapers v. Whalen,* 69 NY2d 246 (1987).
4. *Ibid.,* p. 254.
5. Public Officers Law §87(2)(a).
6. 20 USC §1232g. For a further discussion of FERPA, see part 3.
7. 34 *Code of Federal Regulations* (hereafter cited as CFR) §99.37.
8. Education Law §6510(b).
9. *Murphy v. State Education Department,* 148 AD2d 160, 163-64 (1st Dept. 1989).
10. Public Officers Law §87(2)(b).
11. *Ibid.,* §89(2)(b).
12. *Ibid.,* §89(2)(c).
13. See, e.g., *Matter of Gannett Co., Inc., v. County of Monroe,* 59 AD2d 309 (4th Dept. 1977), *aff'd* 45 NY2d 954 (1978); *Sinicropi v. County of Nassau,* 76 AD2d 838 (1st Dept. 1980); *Geneva Printing Company and Donald Hadley v. Village of Lyons,* unreported (Sup. Ct., Wayne Co. 1981); *Capital Newspapers v. Burns,* 67 NY2d 562 (1986).
14. See, e.g., *Matter of Wool,* unreported (Sup. Ct., Nassau Co. 1977).
15. *Steinmetz v. Board of Education, East Moriches,* unreported (Sup. Ct., Suffolk Co. 1980).
16. *Ibid.*
17. *Matter of Pooler v. Nyquist,* 89 Misc. 2d 705, 708-10 (1976).
18. See, e.g., *Capital Newspapers v. Burns,* 67 NY2d 562, 566-67 (1986); *Village Times, Inc., v. Three Village CSD,* unreported (Sup. Ct., Suffolk Co. 1983); and *Harris v. Baruch College,* 114 AD2d 805 (1st Dept. 1985).
19. *Gannett News Service, Inc., v. State Office of Alcoholism and Substance Abuse,* 99 Misc. 2d 235 (Sup. Ct., Albany Co. 1979).
20. *Cornell University v. City of New York Police Department,* 153 AD2d 515 (1st Dept. 1989).
21. Public Officers Law §87(2)(e).
22. Education Law §3020-a(3)(c); 8 NYCRR §82.9.
23. *Herald Company v. School District of the City of Syracuse,* 104 Misc. 2d 1041, 1046 (1980).
24. *Ibid.,* 104 Misc. 2d 1045 (1980).
25. *Buffalo Evening News, Inc., v. Board of Education of the Hamburg Central School District* (Sup. Ct., Erie Co. 1987).
26. *Ibid.,* p. 4.
27. *Geneva Printing Company and Donald Hadley v. Village of Lyons,* unreported (Sup. Ct., Wayne Co. 1981).

28. Freedom of Information Law-Advisory Opinion (hereafter cited as FOIL-AO)-5910 (January 18, 1990).

29. *Police Association v. Pension Fund*, 61 NY2d 6590, 661 (1983).

30. Laws of 1983, chap. 783; Public Officers Law §89(7).

31. Public Officers Law §89(2)(b)(iii).

32. *Matter of Buffalo Teachers Federation v. Buffalo Board of Education*, 156 AD2d 1027, 1028 (4th Dept. 1989).

33. Public Officers Law §87(2)(c).

34. *Cohalan v. Board of Education of Bayport-Bluepoint School District*, 74 AD2d 812 (1st Dept. 1980).

35. *Matter of Doolan v. BOCES*, 48 NY2d 341, 346-47 (1979).

36. Public Officers Law §87(2)(d).

37. *Matter of Belth v. Insurance Department*, 95 Misc. 2d 118 (Sup. Ct., New York Co. 1977).

38. *Ibid.*, p. 120.

39. Public Officers Law §87(2)(e).

40. *Matter of Fink v. Lefkowitz*, 47 NY2d 567 (1979).

41. *Ibid.*, 573.

42. *Matter of Allen v. Strojnowski*, 129 AD2d 700 (2d Dept. 1987), *motion for leave to appeal denied* 70 NY2d 871 (1987); see Public Officers Law §87(2)(e)(i), (iii).

43. Public Officers Law §87(2)(f).

44. *Matter of Stronza v. Hoke*, 148 AD2d 900 (3d Dept. 1989).

45. *Ibid.*, p. 901.

46. Public Officers Law §87(2)(g).

47. *Ibid.*, §87(g)(i-iv).

48. *Shaw v. Lerer*, 446 NY

49. *Matter of Dunlea v. Goldmark*, 43 NY2d 754, 755 (1977).

50. *Ibid.*, 54 AD2d 446, 449 (3d Dept. 1976).

51. *Ibid.*, p. 449.

52. *Golubski v. Quinones*, unreported (Sup. Ct., King Co. 1985).

53. FOIL-AO-3760 (June 12, 1985).

54. *Geneva Printing Co. v. South Seneca School District* (Sup. Ct., Monroe Co. 1982).

55. *Matter of McAulay v. Board of Education, City of New York*, 61 AD2d 1048 (2d Dept. 1978), *aff'd* 48 NY2d 660 (1979).

56. *Sinicropi v. County of Nassau*, 76 AD2d 832, 833 (1st Dept. 1980).

57. *Russo v. Nassau Community College*, 554 NYS2d 774, 775-77 (1982).

58. *Miller v. Hewlett-Woodmere Union Free School District*, unreported (Sup. Ct., Nassau Co. 1990).

59. *Matter of Kheel v. Ravitch*, 62 NY2d 1, 2-3 (1984).

60. *Xerox Corp. v. Town of Webster*, 65 NY2d 131, 133 (1985).

61. Public Officers Law §87(2)(h).

62. *Local 371 v. Cunningham*, 109 Misc. 2d 331, 337-40 (1981), *aff'd* 90 AD2d 696 (1st Dept. 1982).

63. Public Officers Law §87(2)(i).

64. FOIL-AO-3760 (June 12, 1985).

65. *Ibid.*, p. 2.

66. *Cirale v. 80 Pine Street Corporation,* 35 NY2d 113 (1974); see also Freeman, Robert J., "A Primer on New York's Freedom of Information Law," *New York Law Journal* (Feb. 25, 1983).

67. *Matter of Doolan v. Board of Cooperative Educational Services,* 48 NY2d 341, 347 (1979).

68. *Geneva Printing Company and Donald Hadley v. Village of Lyons,* unreported (Sup. Ct., Wayne Co. 1981).

69. *Ibid.*, p. 5. See, e.g., *Cirale v. 80 Pine Street Corporation,* 35 NY2d 113 (1974); *Farrell v. Village Board of Trustees of the Village of Johnson City,* 83 Misc. 2d 125 (1975); *Young v. Town of Huntington,* 88 Misc. 2d 632 (1976).

70. Public Officers Law §87(2)(b).

71. *Ibid.*, §§87(2)(b), 89(2).

72. *Matter of Farbman & Sons, Inc., v. New York City Health and Hospitals Corporation,* 62 NY2d 75, 80-82 (1984).

73. *Ibid.*, see also CPLR §3120 and Public Officers Law §89(3).

Chapter 11.   Procedures for Accessing Records

1. Public Officers Law §89(3).

2. *Lecker v. New York City Board of Education,* 157 AD2d 486, 487 (1st Dept. 1990).

3. *Matter of Farbman & Sons, Inc., v. New York City Health & Hospitals Corporation,* 62 NY2d 75, 83 (1984).

4. *Matter of Dunlea v. Goldmark,* 85 Misc. 2d 198, 1990201 (1976), *aff'd* 54 AD2d 446 (3d Dept. 1976), *aff'd* 43 NY2d 754 (1977).

5. *Matter of Gannett Co., Inc., v. County of Monroe,* 59 AD2d 309 (4th Dept. 1977).

6. *Ibid.*, pp. 312-13.

Chapter 12.   The Appeal Process

1. Public Officers Law §89(4)(b); see also *Appeal of O'Dell,* ___Ed. Dept. Rep.___(March 28, 1991); *Appeal of Alexandreena D.,* 30 *ibid.* 303; *Appeal of Krasinski,* 29 *ibid.* 375; *Appeal of Zook,* 28 *ibid.* 77.

2. Public Officers Law §89(4)(b).

3. *Ibid.*, §89(4)(a).

4. *Ibid.*, §89(5)(d).

5. *Matter of Floyd v. McGuire,* 87 AD2d 388, 390 (1st Dept. 1982).

6. Public Officers Law §89(4)(b).

7. *Matter of Fink v. Lefkowitz,* 47 NY2d 567, 571 (1979); *Farbman & Sons, Inc., v. New York City Health and Hospitals Corporation,* 62 NY2d 75, 80 (1984); *Capital Newspapers v. Burns,* 67 NY2d 562, 566 (1986).

8. Public Officers Law §89(4)(c).

9. *Powhida v. City of Albany*, 147 AD2d 236, 239 (3d Dept. 1989); *Friedland v. Maloney*, 148 AD2d 814, 815 (3d Dept. 1989).
10. Penal Law §240.65.
11. *Matter of Pooler v. Nyquist*, 89 Misc. 2d 705, 709-10; *Miracle Mile Associates v. Yudelson*, 68 AD2d 176, 180 (4th Dept. 1979).

Chapter 13. Management, Retention and Destruction of Records

1. Arts and Cultural Affairs Law, Article 57-A.
2. 8 NYCRR §185.2[c].
3. *Ibid.*, §185.4[b]. The current schedule promulgated by the commissioner is Schedule Ed-1 (1988).
4. *Ibid.*, §185.6.
5. *Ibid.*, §185.

Part 3. The Family Educational Rights and Privacy Act

Chapter 14. Introduction

1. 20 USC §1232g.
2. 20 USC §1232g[g]; See chap. 17 for a more complete discussion of enforcement under the Family Educational Rights and Privacy Act (hereafter referred to as FERPA).
3. The final regulations implementing FERPA were promulgated by the secretary of health, education and welfare on June 17, 1976. The Department of Health, Education and Welfare (HEW) was originally granted the act's rule-making authority and charged with administrative responsibility for it. This responsibility is now vested in the secretary of the Department of Education, and the regulations are located at 34 CFR §99.1 *et seq.* To obtain a copy of these regulations, one should request 34 CFR Part 99.

Chapter 15. Rights of Parents and Eligible Students

1. 34 CFR §99.5.
2. Among the funded programs not covered by FERPA, include the High School Equivalency Program and College Assistance Migrant Program, programs administered by the commissioner of the Rehabilitation Services Administration and the directors of the National Institute on Disability and Rehabilitation Research, the Transition Program for Refugee Children, and several programs administered by the assistant secretary for educational research and improvement.

3. 34 CFR §99.1.

4. *Ibid.*, §99.3 [a].

5. *Ibid.*, §99.3; 20 USC §1232g [4] [B] [i].

6. See *School-based Student Assistance Programs: Reconciling Federal Regulations under the Family Educational Rights and Privacy Act and the Alcohol and Drug Abuse Confidentiality Statutes*, opinion issued jointly by the Alcohol, Drug Abuse and Mental Health Administration; the U. S. Department of Health and Human Services; and the Family Policy Compliance Office, U. S. Department of Education, Sept. 25, 1990.

7. 34 CFR §99.3; 20 USC §1232g [4] [B] [ii].

8. 34 CFR §99.3; 20 USCA §1232g [4] [B] [iii].

9. 34 CFR §99.3.

10. *Ibid.*

11. *Klein Independent School Dist. v. Mattox*, 830 F2d 576 [5th Cir; 1987].

12. 34 CFR §99.3.

13. *Ibid.*; 20 USC §1232g [4] [B] [iv].

14. 34 CFR §99.3.

15. FOIL-AO-6108 (June 4, 1990).

16. *Ibid.*, p. 7.

17. *Ibid.* See also FOIL-AO-6279 (Oct. 2, 1990) on this issue.

18. FOIL-AO-6108; June 4, 1990, p. 8.

19. 34 CFR §99.3; 20 USC §1232g [a] [5] [A].

20. *Ibid.*, §99.30[a].

21. *Ibid.*, §99.30 [b], [c] [1], [c] [2].

22. *Ibid.*, §99.31 [a] [1]; 20 USC §1232g [b] [1] [a]; U. S. Department of Education Fact Sheet.

23. Memorandum from Gerald Freeborne, deputy commissioner, Office of Elementary, Secondary and Continuing Education, and Basil Y. Scott, deputy commissioner, Office of Vocational Rehabilitation, State Education Department, to superintendents of public and non-public schools, January 17, 1983.

24. 34 CFR §§99.31[1] [2], 99.34.

25. *Ibid.*, §99.34[a] [3].

26. *Ibid.*, §99.34[b] [2].

27. *Ibid.*, §99.31[a] [3] [i], [ii], [iii].

28. *Matter of Board of Education (City of New York) v. Regan*, 131 Misc. 2d 514, 515-16 (1986). The court also held that there was no statute predating 1974 that would have required the names of the students to be disclosed (*ibid.*, p. 516). FERPA provides an exception to confidentiality when the records are sought by "state and local officials or authorities to whom such information is specifically required to be reported or disclosed pursuant to State statute adopted prior to November 19, 1974" (20 USC §1232g [b] [1] [e]; also see "Release of Records without Consent," p. 74).

29. *Matter of Board of Education (City of New York) v. Regan*, 131 Misc. 2d 516. p. 516.

30. 34 CFR §99.35 [a]; 20 USC §1232g [b] [5].

31. 34 CFR §99.35.
32. *Ibid.*, §99.31 [a] [4] [i].
33. *Ibid.*, §99.31 [a] [5] [i].
34. *Ibid.*, §99.31 [a] [6].
35. *Ibid.*, §99.31 [a] [7].
36. See, e.g., 26 USC §152 and 34 CFR §99.31.
37. 34 CFR §99.31 [a] [9] [i], [iii].
38. *Ibid.*, §99.31 [a] [10]; 20 USC §1232g [b] [i] [h].
39. 34 CFR §99.36.
40. Education Law §3209-a.
41. *Ibid.*
42. Social Services Law §413 [1]. The Child Abuse Prevention and Treatment Act of 1974 requires states to adopt legislation providing immunity for those reporting suspected child abuse (42 USCA Chapter 67).
43. Education Law §3028-a.
44. 34 CFR §99.10 [f]; 20 USC §1232g [4] [B] [iv].
45. Mary H. B. Gelfman and Nadine C. Schwab, "School Health Services and Educational Records: Conflicts in the Law," 64 Educ. Law. Rep. 319, 321.
46. See *School-based Student Assistance Programs: Reconciling Federal Regulations under the Family Educational Rights and Privacy Act and the Alcohol and Drug Abuse Confidentiality Statutes,* opinion issued jointly by the Alcohol, Drug Abuse and Mental Health Administration, U. S. Department of Health and Human Services and the Family Policy Compliance Office, U. S. Department of Education, Sept. 25, 1990.
47. *Ibid.*, p. 3.
48. "Capacity to consent" is based upon the individual's ability to understand and appreciate the nature and consequences of health care service, not on the age of the student; Public Health Law §§2780 (5), 2783.
49. 34 CFR §99.31 [a] [11].
50. 34 CFR §99.37 [a] [1]; §99.3.
51. *Matter of Krauss (Nassau Community College),* 122 Misc. 2d 218 (1983). It is interesting that the court also stated the college properly refused the information under New York State's Freedom of Information Law, based apparently on FOIL's denial of access exemption for records that "are specifically exempted from disclosure by state or federal statute" (Public Officers Law §87 [2] [a], see also 122 Misc. 2d, 220). In addition, because the court found the students had a right to privacy, the college also could deny the request under section 87 [2] [b] of FOIL, "particularly since petitioner has failed to show that the names and addresses are not sought for 'commercial or fund-raising purposes'" under §89 [2] [b] [iii] of FOIL (see 122 Misc. 2d, 220).
52. *Kestenbaum v. Michigan State University,* 294 NY2d 228, 233, *aff'd* 327 NY2d 783 [1980].
53. *Education Week,* 10, no. 19 (Jan. 30, 1991): 1.
54. 34 CFR §99.37 [a] [2], [a] [3].

55. 34 CFR §99.37 [b]; see *Kestenbaum v. Michigan State University*, 294 NY2d 228, *aff'd* 327 NY2d 783 [1980]; *Matter of Krauss*, 122 Misc. 2d 218 [1983].

56. 34 CFR §99.31[b].

57. *Matter of Kryston v. Board of Education (East Ramapo Central School District)*, 77 AD2d 896 [2d Dept. 1980].

58. *Ibid.*, p. 897; see also Public Officers Law §89 [3]. The court cited to *Matter of Miracle Mile Association v. Yudelson*, 68 AD2d 176, 181; and *Vaughn v. Rosen*, 484 F2d 820, 823. It is interesting that the court stated FERPA provides maximum access to documents. Although this may be true in regard to directory information, it is certainly not the intent in regard to third parties' access to personally identifiable information.

59. *Sauerhof v. City of New York*, 108 Misc 2d 805 [1981].

60. *Ibid.*, pp. 806-8.

61. 34 CFR §99.3 [a] [1]; §99.33 [a] [2].

62. *Ibid.*, §99.33 [b] [1], [2].

63. *Ibid.*, §99.33 [c].

64. *Ibid.*, §99.10 [b]; 20 USC §1232g [a] [1] [A].

65. 34 CFR §99.10 [c].

66. Public Officers Law §89 (3).

67. Rights of Non-custodial Parents, U. S. Department of Education.

68. Public Officers Law §87 (2).

69. See 34 CFR 99.11 [a]; *Ibid.*, §99.6 [a] [2] [iii]; Public Officers Law §87 (1) (b) [iii].

70. 34 CFR §99.12 [a].

71. *Ibid.*, §99.20 [a].

72. *Ibid.*, §99.20 [b] and [c].

73. EHLR Special Report: Family Rights and Privacy Discussion on §99.21.

74. CFR §99.21 [a]; 20 USC §1232g [a] [2].

75. 34 CFR §99.22 [a].

76. *Ibid.*, §99.22 [b].

77. *Ibid.*, §99.22 [c].

78. *Ibid.*, §99.22 [d].

79. *Ibid.*, §99.22 [e].

80. *Ibid.*, §99.22 [f].

81. *Ibid.*, §99.21 [b] [1], [2].

82. *Ibid.*, §99.21 [c].

83. *Ibid.*, §99.4.

84. Rights of Non-custodial Parents, U. S. Department of Education.

85. See *Matter of Page v. Rotterdam-Mohonasen Central School District*, 109 Misc. 2d 1049 [1981].

86. Rights of Non-custodial Parents, U. S. Department of Education.

87. *Ibid.*

88. *Fay v. South Colonie Central School District*, 802 F2d 21 [1986].

89. *Ibid.*, p. 34.

90. *Ibid.*, p. 24.

Chapter 16. The Board of Education's Responsibilities

1. 34 CFR §99.6 [b].
2. *Ibid.*, §99.6 [a] [1].
3. *Ibid.*, §99.6 [a] [2].
4. *Ibid.*, §99.6 [a] [2] [i], [ii], [iii], [iv].
5. *Ibid.*, §99.12 [a]. For a more detailed discussion of these issues, see "Inspection and Review," p. 80.
6. 34 CFR §99.6 [a] [3].
7. *Ibid.*, §99.6 [a] [4].
8. *Ibid.*, §99.6 [a] [5].
9. *Ibid.*, §99.6 [a] [6].
10. *Ibid.*, §99.6 [a] [7].
11. 20 USC §1232g [e]; 34 CFR §99.7 [a], [a] [1], [2], [3], [4], [5], [5] [b], [c].
12. *Ibid.*, §99.7 [a] [5] [d]; see also *Rios v. Read*, 73 FRD 589 [EDNY, 1977]. In Rios, the court held that the Spanish-speaking parents and students were entitled to appropriate notice in both English and Spanish.
13. 34 CFR §99.32 [a] [1], [2].
14. *Ibid.*, §99.32 [a] [3] [i], [ii].
15. *Ibid.*, §99.32 [b] [1], [2].
16. *Ibid.*, §99.32 [c], [d].
17. *Ibid.*, §99.10 [e]; Rights of Non-custodial Parents, U. S. Department of Education.

Chapter 17. Enforcement Procedures

1. 20 USC §1232g [g]; 34 CFR §99.60 [a], [b], [c].
2. *Ibid.*, § 99.61.
3. *Ibid.*, §99.64 [a], [b].
4. *Ibid.*, §99.65 [a], [b] [1], [2].
5. *Ibid.*, §99.66 [a].
6. *Ibid.*, §99.66 [b], [c] [1], [2].
7. *Ibid.*, §99.67 [b].
8. *Ibid.*, §99.67 [a] [1], [2], [3].
9. *Ibid.*, §§78.2 [b], 78.6 [b]. This includes almost all programs administered by the department.
10. See, for example, *Klein Independent School District v. Mattox*, 830 F2d 576 [1987]; *Fay v. South Colonie Central School District*, 802 F2d 21 [1986]; *Smith v. Duquesne University*, 612 F Supp 77 [1985], *aff'd* 787 F2d 583 [1986].
11. *Fay v. South Colonie* 802 F2d 21 [1986].
12. *Ibid.*, p. 33.

Chapter 18. Other Relevant Federal and State Laws and Regulations

1. 20 USC §1400 *et seq.*
2. *Ibid.*, §1415, 1415 [b].
3. *Ibid.*, §§1418 [b], 1417 [c].
4. 34 CFR §§300.560 et seq., 300.561 [a] [3].
5. *Ibid.*, §300.561 [a] [4].
6. *Ibid.*, §300.562 [a].
7. See, for example, *Ibid.*, §§99.10 [b], §300.562 [a].
8. *Ibid.*, §§300.562 [b] [3] [c], 99.4; see also "Rights of Non-custodial Parents," p. 82.
9. *Ibid.*, 34 CFR §§300.562-570.
10. *Ibid.*, §300.571 [a] [1], [2], [b].
11. *Ibid.*, §300.571 [c].
12. *Ibid.*, §300.572 [a], [b], 2 [c], [d].
13. *Ibid.*, §300.573 [a], [b]. One comment on this regulation suggests that although destruction of records is the best way to ensure against improper and unauthorized disclosure, districts should inform parents that such records may be needed for Social Security benefits or other purposes.
14. 34 CFR §§300.574, 99.44 [a].
15. 8 NYCRR §200.7 [3] [2].